THEATRE IN THE ROUND

STEPHEN JOSEPH

Theatre in the Round

113578

TAPLINGER PUBLISHING COMPANY
NEW YORK

First Published in the United States in 1968 by
TAPLINGER PUBLISHING CO., INC.
29 East Tenth Street
New York, New York 10003

Library of Congress Catalog Card Number 68-17640

Printed in Great Britain

For
WILLIAM ELMHIRST

Contents

List of Photographs

1
Argument

THEATRE in the round is one particular kind of theatre. In this book I shall attempt to describe what I have learned about it, and, in order to do so, will compare it with other forms of theatre. There is a danger here. I am an enthusiast, and may let my enthusiasm run over so that my remarks about other kinds of theatre are unfair. This danger is increased because, now that people here and there are trying to decide how to build the ideal theatre (to serve, perhaps, as a civic theatre), there is a good deal of setting one kind of theatre up against another, and everyone is almost forced to take sides, though I, for one, do not want to do so. So let me state my belief in the simple fact that there is plenty of room for all kinds of theatre; indeed, we urgently need more theatres, and the more kinds the better.

There is no need to be tolerant of everything. I have just been into a small theatre (there must be hundreds like it all over this country), a hall, not originally intended to be a theatre, with a flat auditorium floor that gives very bad sightlines to a raised stage at one end, behind a proscenium arch. The ceiling is at the same level all over, so the height over the stage is inadequate for scenery. The stage is rigged with untidy wings and borders of grey drill material. The plaster wall at the back is painted pale blue and has a horizontal band of dirty handmarks, a few patches knocked out of the plaster, and some heavy scratches where the tops of flats have knocked against it. The sets of lines have been wrongly coiled on cleats, and most of the ends have been long frayed, some of them have been partially plaited, and several have been cut short (making them useless). I cannot be tolerant of this. Much could be improved if the people using this hall knew how to use their equipment, though when you meet them they only complain that they do not have enough equipment. In my opinion they already have too much. They do not know how to use it properly. And it is the wrong sort of equipment. But even if the plaster back wall were clean and new, and the lines were properly finished and tied off on the cleats, even if the thing were properly maintained, I should still question the validity of this hall. To me it does not make sense. What is it really for? If among the many people who use this hall there are a handful who want to act, is this kind of structure sensible? I think not. There are three reasons against it.

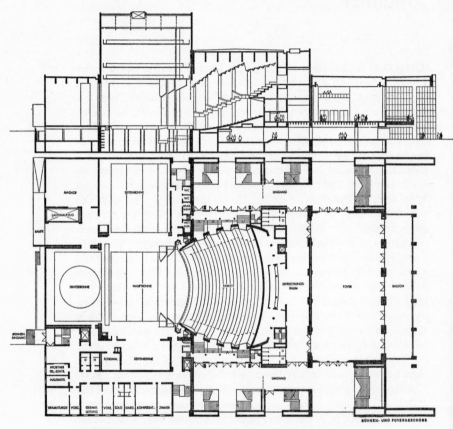

1. Plan and section of the new theatre at Recklinghausen. It is a conventional proscenium theatre and in England, where we imitate the type, it would probably occupy a fiftieth of the space, cost a fiftieth of the price and be without the facilities that properly belong to such a theatre. We can only plead that the Germans build opera houses while we, supposedly, build playhouses.

Firstly, the people who use it, as the condition it is now in proclaims, do not know how to use it. Secondly, it is an imitation of the conventional proscenium theatre without the real facilities that belong to such a theatre; for instance, the main object of the proscenium is to conceal the spaces backstage where scenery is stacked and shifted and to hide the machinery used for moving scenery, but this theatre scarcely uses scenery and finds itself in the paradoxical situation of having to put up curtains on stage to hide the backstage spaces. The plaster back wall is only an imitation cyclorama which has few of the uses of a proper cyclorama. This hall would serve its particular purpose if it were a lot simpler, if the equipment were installed for a real purpose instead of a purpose which requires better equipment. Thirdly, even if the theatre were fully equipped, as some of the people who use it clearly wish, and if it were then properly maintained and run, it would be far too complicated for its purpose which is for amateur actors, for occasional performances, and far too expensive for them to run and maintain. If you consider this hall and its purpose you must begin to search for basic principles: what is a theatre for? And this question soon brings you face to face with the fact that there are many kinds of theatre, and that the one function they have in common is to provide a space where actors may act in front of an audience. This is the essential requirement of any theatre, and we should turn it over in our minds carefully. It is possible and, in my opinion, desirable to build many theatres very simply, without a lot of technical apparatus, admirably suited to the purpose of the hall now under criticism, and of the huge number of halls like it.

Simplicity is appropriate only for certain theatres. A large professional company, with many experienced actors and technicians, may justifiably demand the best that can be obtained. When I go to a theatre like the new Nottingham Playhouse, I rejoice. But it took a long time for Nottingham to get that magnificent theatre, and there are many towns that have not yet started on their spadework. Besides, no one would expect jewels like this to be common. So I dismiss Nottingham, and get on with things at mud level. Many, many theatre enterprises of importance have begun modestly. Peter Godfrey and Norman Marshall at the little Gate Theatre in London (both its premises very unlikely as theatres); J. B. Fagan at the Oxford Playhouse. The long history of the theatre contains many stories of grand results from small seeds. I am in favour of small beginnings, and I am very strongly in favour of small theatres. But I do not want to pull big theatres down (provided they are serving some useful function). Nor do I exclude the possibility that small theatres, which I am at the moment concerned with, may flourish and grow. But let us never lose sight of simplicity and essentials.

Acting, then, is the primary business of the theatre. Actors initiate the drama. Next come audiences. We can stop there. We have got most of what is important. Playwrights, producers and so on are, comparatively, of secondary importance. Acting is a creative art, and it is a social art. And it seems to me that if we use this art well (as mostly we do not) it can be both an enjoyable and a valuable experience. What I mean by this is complicated, and I can best throw light on the idea by extending the accepted concept of child play (which is a means of helping children through imitation and exploration to become adults) so that it leads to the proposition that adults themselves in a fully realised theatre are helped to become socially more mature. This claim needs a good deal of justifying if only because there is so little sign of it; we do not have anything like a fully developed theatre, we do not use well the art of acting, we have let our theatre become over-refined, rarefied, literary, superficial, impoverished. The way back to a more vigorous theatre lies through a consideration of essentials; a fresh evaluation of acting and of theatres.

It follows that I am as concerned with amateur acting as with professional acting and with the amateur theatre as much as the professional theatre. I wish the professional theatre would lead the way to a more exciting and popular dramatic art, but if it doesn't (and it doesn't seem like doing so at present) then there is no harm in describing the opportunities to anyone who may be interested, amateur companies in particular. The word amateur has, unfortunately, in the theatre become almost pejorative. I do not ever mean to use it in this sense. It is true that some amateurs in our theatre tend to look upon the business of theatre in too lighthearted and casual a way; but if I accuse them, I offer them the excuse too that they are set just such an example by many professional actors. There are times when one despairs of the profession. It is vastly overcrowded; every other person thinks that if only he were given a good part and a good producer, he would be better than Olivier; too few actors have a wide range of performing skills; the organisation and administration of theatre is so hopelessly muddled and inefficient that an intelligent person is almost inevitably driven out; it is truly the stupidest profession of them all. Yet the theatre has a tremendous attraction; we perceive its latent powers and persevere. Truly talented artists put up with all the folly, they work hard, and, few as they are, continue to give us encouragement. We are optimistic. At best, amateurs are those who love the theatre, work hard at it, have skill and talent, and differ from the professionals only in that they do not earn their livings in the theatre. I have met enough of them for me to suspect that they may well take the opportunity that is always before them, and show us the full vigour and fun of the theatre.

Theatre in the round is still little used, most people seem to prefer big theatres to small ones, the actor (however important as a star) is at present usually less considered than the playwright or the producer, and the amateur actor is seldom thought capable of contributing to the artistic riches of the theatre (except where he is anyhow on the brink of becoming a professional). I do not share the general view on these topics, but I enjoy discussing them; though I am not always sure if the people I am talking to will be shocked by the unorthodoxy of my standpoint, or distressed by the inconsistency of my arguments. I usually bring more than a touch of prejudice to whatever I am working at, and nothing deserves other people's contempt more than one's own prejudice.

When I first saw Jack Mitcheley's company performing in the round, I was absolutely delighted; as far as I could see most of the other people in the audience on that occasion were also delighted. The many performances that I saw in the round in the United States added to my growing enthusiasm. In 1955, when I started a small professional theatre in the round in England, it didn't seem to me to be very sensational to do so because it was such an easy and straightforward way of enjoying acting and plays. However, I did believe that within a few years there would be dozens more such theatres; I was wrong about this. Further, to my great surprise the idea of a central stage received a good deal of rough handling from writers and critics. Most of the criticism that has been levelled against the idea is purely theoretical, if only because there is not yet in England a proper theatre in the round where one can see exactly what this form of theatre is capable of. Anyone who rejects the idea after witnessing a performance or two in Scarborough or in Stoke is not being fair to his own standards; he would hesitate to assess the potentialities of the enclosed stage after watching a performance in a school gymnasium. The idea, then, still attracts me. I cannot do more than offer an opinion about the fact (as opposed to the idea) and I daresay some of the rude remarks that have been made about my own productions in the round are more than justified. All I can offer in defence is that I do my best; though I have not taken the major creative responsibility for more than a small proportion of the plays presented by the Studio Theatre company. Most of the productions by this company, and other companies here and abroad that I have seen on the central stage, seem to me no better and certainly no worse than one would expect in any form of theatre. No, that is too apologetic; I really do enjoy watching performances on a centre stage more than on any other form of stage. Why? I will try to sort out the reasons.

The theatre has always been influenced by changing fashions. There is little that is absolutely permanent about it (and precisely what that little consists of has provided us with a perennial debate), while obviously the most noticeable aspects of theatre are wholly ephemeral. The actors exit from the stage, leaving nothing behind them but a few memories. The brief hour or two of performance serves to remind us in little of the mysterious brevity of our own lives, but it is fact we take little pleasure in; we cannot escape it, though we can disguise it. So we strive for permanent values, in life and in the theatre. The playwright tries, from time to time, to plumb the depths of time's mystery and to answer the riddle of existence, and in the audience we may glimpse, during a performance of *King Lear* perhaps, what he has proposed for our comfort. And at least the play script survives for us to read. This is something as nearly permanent as the theatre can offer, and it is not surprising that many knowledgeable people make the mistake of supposing that the written play is the essence of the theatre; but when we examine the plays that have survived from the earliest of times to the present, we cannot help noticing that even the business of writing plays is subject to fashion. A play by Aeschylus is different from a play by Shakespeare; a play by Molière is different from a play by Noel Coward. Not just because the writers were different people, but rather because a playwright works within the conventions of his theatre, and these conventions are mutable.

The conventions of the theatre, of its literary style and content as well as its physical and architectural form, reflect the life of the time; but in our efforts to halt the passing moment we find ourselves hanging on to yesterday's conventions. We try to turn them into permanent precepts and rules. Of course we fail. The attempt runs counter to the nature of drama, and finally manifests itself in a quarrel between those who cling to old conventions, who want to retain the old and familiar kind of theatre, and those who are advocating something new. As far as buildings are concerned, on the one hand there is the established theatre with its auditorium facing a proscenium arch, behind which is the stage house, and on the other hand a host of alternatives—most of them with the stage or acting area in the same room as the auditorium. Theatre in the round, an extreme form of open stage, can be looked on as an enemy to the conventional theatre. It may be so, but it is a question that only the future can decide. I believe the many different sorts of theatre can exist side by side until whichever has served its purpose goes out of fashion and is no longer used.

The theatre reached a golden age at the end of the last century, and has since been diminished first by the cinema and then by television. In order to fight back the theatre should present a united front, perhaps. But the golden age was a golden age of bricks and mortar, commercial profits and spectacular shows; the last attracted a huge public that soon found their moving pictures better done in the cinema. Fair enough. The bricks and mortar, no matter how glorious some of these theatres were (and still are), do not seem to me to be important claimants for permanence. Most buildings go out of fashion, though some are always worth preserving for historical interest. Theatres too. But we might show our strength in a more positive policy. If old theatres are no longer useful, pull them down. If theatres are threatened, it would seem to be sensible to fight back by building new theatres. But we are prevented from doing this by thought of commercial profits. At present it is by no means a good investment to build a theatre. In which case we ought, perhaps, to persuade municipal authorities to build them; though, in this matter as in so many others, the municipal authorities are likely to be more old-fashioned than businessmen of the theatrical profession itself.

During the years that followed World War II, many theatres were pulled down. An advocate of theatre in the round may well say; let them go. And isn't this destructive? Isn't this a misplaced iconoclasm that can only weaken the theatre as a whole? Well, if it is then the theatre is a very feeble affair indeed and nothing is likely to save it; though a few transfusions (from the Arts Council?) may keep it artificially alive for a little while longer. But I cannot subscribe to such a pessimistic notion. Not much is really at stake when an old theatre is pulled down; if there are audiences and actors in the neighbourhood the important thing is to build a new theatre. There's the rub.

Whenever a new theatre is contemplated, I hope that the idea of a theatre in the round will be seriously considered, even though it is not at present to everyone's liking. For how can people know whether or not they will like theatre in the round until they have seen it? How will they ever see it if every municipal authority that builds a theatre has to play safe and build a form of theatre that has already proved itself? The answer may have to be that energetic individuals must carry the burden of enterprise, of experiment and of exploration. It may have to be done in a small way; converted warehouses or cinemas, temporary adaptations of unlikely spaces, garages, kitchens. Then comes the cry: why should an individual force his particular idea of theatre on other people? This leads me to my escape clause in arguing with people who do not like theatre in the round; they are entitled to their view. I do not want to convince them in advance that theatre in the round is good, though I do want to offer it to as many people as possible so that they can see it and make up their own minds. Further, I do not want to base any argument on a monopoly or a superlative. Not for me to suggest that every theatre ought to be a theatre in the round; on the contrary, if I attack the proscenium theatre it is because it has virtually that monopoly. And I would be the first to criticise any form of theatre that now claimed a better right to this stranglehold. Besides, I don't see that theatre in the round need claim that it is the *best* form of theatre, nor that it is better than another form—even the proscenium stage. If theatre in the round can prove that it provides some people with good entertainment, that is enough. Theatre should be a rich diet of good things. We can best develop our tastes if we have a wide range of things to sample. The more different sorts of theatre, the better, say I. Which brings us back to where we started.

This book is not written for experts. It is written for people who are beginning to take an interest in the theatre. I hope what I have described here will enable the youngest of Youth Groups or Women's Institutes drama sections to get on with the business of acting in the round: without having to use big theatres, without having to spend large sums of money. But once you have begun, it is difficult to be quite sure where to stop and I have carried on the technical information to a point where it may be useful to a small professional company. Indeed it comes from my own experience of dealing with just such an enterprise.

Do not expect instant success just because you may be venturing on something comparatively new. If you try a performance in the round, certainly good friends will tell you precisely what was wrong with it. But immediate or occasional success or failure prove nothing. Even a famous producer, for example, Peter Brook, can produce a great actor, such as Sir John Gielgud, in a marvellous play, for instance *The Tempest*, at an established theatre, like Drury Lane, and the whole show may be fairly dismal. We do not on this account conclude that picture-frame stages are no use, nor that they are unsuitable for staging this sort of play, nor even that the performance might have been more successful on another form of stage.

It is an odd fact about theatre that very few people have much use for it, yet those who do become acquainted with it so often develop into devotees. Having become enraptured, and being a minority, they are tempted to form a secret society whose privileges are not to be shared among common people. This applies to amateur groups who spend long hours at their arcane labours and to professional theatre people who seem to live in a private world that is only occasionally punctured by outrageous reports in popular newspapers. But I see no reason why the theatre should not be as popular as football, why it should not provide social activity as free and easy as that we find every day in the pub, why it should not be as accessible as fish and chips, and much more enjoyable. In any discussion of the theatre the public tends to get left out. It must be brought back.

I have sat in many theatres, watching many plays, and have often felt that the whole proceedings was intended for a non-existent audience. Indeed, audiences in playhouses are at best only a very small proportion of the population. Supposedly theatre is a popular art; and television and cinema do have large audiences. The potential audience for the playhouse stays away. What can we do about it? What can we do to get a bigger audience? Don't suppose that I am now asking for bigger theatres; I want more people to come to the theatre, and therefore more theatres, more small theatres—and all of them full. There must obviously be a sensible balance of numbers. The phenomenon of theatre consists of a relatively small group of people (the actors) who act out the events of a story for the entertainment of a much larger group of people (the audience). The larger group, though, must not be so large that some members of the audience cannot see and hear the actors properly.

The order of priorities begins with actors, then audiences, then playwrights—and then theatres to provide walls and a roof so that everyone can find protection from the weather and outside noise.

We are all choosey about the rooms we go into; we might get more people into theatres if there were a wider choice of rooms. But the form of theatre also has an effect upon the actors. Let there also be more variety of acting style; there is nothing certain about the actor's technique, except that it also is subject to changes of fashion. Each great actor, Burbage or Betterton, Garrick or Kean, Irving or Olivier is welcomed because he is more realistic or more true than his immediate predecessors; which is no more than to say that our tastes change and that what our fathers liked is old-fashioned, and that what we like will not suit our children. Is this not what we should expect? The theatre deals with time, and is subject to time's changes.

Starting from the theatre we have today it is sensible to suggest alternatives, improvements, new ideas even. Only a few of them may prove valuable in the actual process of development. And it is probably as well to focus down on to a small section of the whole evolution; to look only as far as tomorrow; to deal only with one small idea. The playhouse is only part of theatre; and within its limits theatre in the round will suffice to take up a good deal of debate.

Finally, it is easy to dismiss theatre in the round as nothing more than the latest fashion. I accept half the implication of this and rejoice in all the exciting changes that are going on in every branch of our theatre; but I question the other half. How can theatre in the round be called a fashion when it scarcely exists? How many such theatres are there in Great Britain? Can you really have a fashionable object without more than one or two examples of it? If any particular form of theatre is fashionable at present, it is the conventional proscenium theatre with a picture-frame stage; there are hundreds of these all over the country. It is true that there is much talk about theatre in the round: talk is certainly fashionable! I am in favour of dismissing the talk and getting on with the job. I do want to see a veritable fashion in theatre in the round. But this does not mean that I expect it to be permanent. That would be stupid. Nor do I expect it to be universal. On the contrary, the competition will be exciting only if there are many other forms of theatre all contending for the crown of fashion. This would give audiences a chance to choose what they like, and in the order of their preference. I don't want to tell audiences or actors what is best for them and deprive them of everything else. So there is a lot of fruitful work to do; new theatres to build, and new audiences to attract, in addition to the consideration of odd ideas.

2
The Early Story

In most discussions about the physical form of the theatre there is considerable looseness in the use of descriptive terms. *Theatre in the round* has been used to describe all sorts of theatre forms. To some people it conjures up images of earnest students in peculiar clothes performing Latvian tragedies to small audiences of eccentric spinsters. To others it means precisely round theatres—such as the new Nottingham Playhouse. Theatre in the round is neither of these things. It is a clumsy term. But there is no obvious alternative, though various alternatives have been widely used; among them *arena theatre* (also much used to describe many other forms of stage), *central staging*, *island staging* and *ring theatre*. None of them is more proof against misuse than *theatre in the round*, and since this term has probably been more used than the others to describe the particular form of theatre with which we are concerned it is reasonable to adopt it and to state as clearly as possible how it is used here.

Theatre in the round, then, is here taken to mean a form of theatre where the audience more or less surrounds a central stage, so that if the actor stands in the middle and turns round he always has as many people behind him as in front of him. Examples include the Arena Theatre in Washington, DC, the *Théâtre en rond* in Paris and the Victoria Theatre in Stoke-on-Trent. The term is not here used to cover theatres with thrust stages such as the Festival Theatre in Chichester, nor end stages as at the Mermaid Theatre in London.

All of these theatres are radically different from the familiar proscenium theatre, which is characterised by its picture-frame stage and the architectural separation of the auditorium space from the stage space. The proscenium theatre has two "houses", divided by the proscenium wall. The stage is enclosed; and this suggests the term *open stage* to describe stages that are in the same architectural space as the auditorium. The various kinds of open stage can

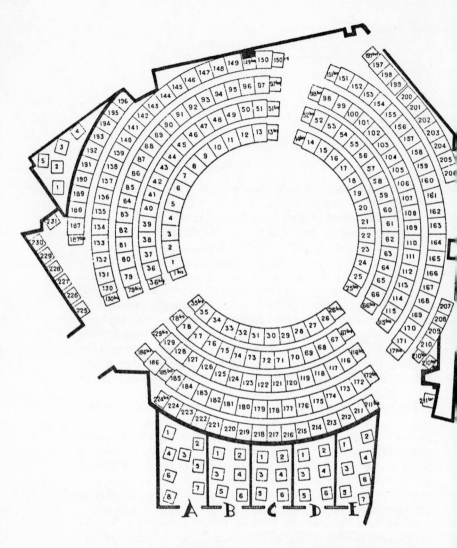

2. *Théâtre en rond* in Paris has a circular seating plan, but, being a conversion from an older building, the theatre walls are pleasantly asymetrical.

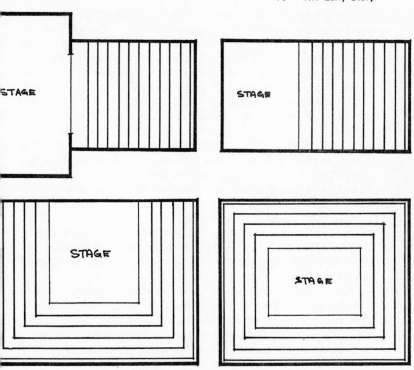

3. Enclosed stage (the conventional proscenium theatre),
and three open stages: end stage, thrust stage and centre
stage. It is the last that we are concerned with here. There
     are many variants and other forms of open stage.

themselves be distinguished by the extent to which the audience em-
braces, as it were, the acting area. If the acting area is considered as a
square, then the end stage has the audience on one side, the thrust
stage on three sides, and theatre in the round on four sides; a *corner
stage* with the audience on two sides is perfectly feasible and something of the sort can be found, for example, in the community theatre
at Western Springs. And a two-sided arrangement of great interest
is the transverse stage, where the acting area is in the middle with
the audience on opposite sides, as at the little Traverse Theatre in

Edinburgh. Few stages are, in fact, square, and there is no limit to the number of stage/auditorium arrangements. Some theatres, such as the Questors at Ealing, deliberately set out to provide for various forms of staging; these are usually called adaptable theatres. Further, every theatre is unique, and it is therefore unwise to be too dogmatic about descriptive terms and categories. However, the idea of theatre in the round can be limited fairly precisely, and it is useful to accept the definitions given here in order to confine the scope of our discussion.

A theatre in the round may have a plan of virtually any shape. The *Théâtre en rond* in Paris is round, the Penthouse Theatre in Washington is elliptical. Square, triangular or irregular shapes are other possibilities. A circular plan is usually assumed to present certain architectural and building difficulties, and to result in acoustic problems. Circular theatres in the round in the United States, such as the Playhouse in Houston, Texas, do not seem to suffer from acoustic problems (but this may only be evidence of the fact that acoustics are different over there). Certainly the three professional theatres in the round in this country have all had rectangular plans, i.e. the theatre in the round at Scarborough, the Pembroke theatre at Croydon and the Victoria Theatre at Stoke. Each of these has been converted from a more or less unsuitable building (and has had acoustic problems). But it follows that, in this country, information and experience are derived mainly from theatres of this shape, and we shall therefore assume a rectangular plan in all discussion that follows unless specially stated.

A theatre in the round may vary in size to accommodate audiences of from less than fifty people to over 2,000. An audience of fifty may be seated in one or two rows; the Casa Mañana in Fort Worth, Texas, accommodates 2,000 in a dozen rows. The smallest audience may be appropriate to an amateur theatre, an experimental theatre, or a private theatre, but a professional company will normally require a larger audience capacity. An audience of 2,000 is appropriate to a theatre presenting musical comedy or opera, as is the case at the Casa Mañana, but this size is probably too big to be sympathetic to the presentation of most modern plays or even to cater for the likely size of audience for such plays. A theatre in the round intended for use as a professional playhouse might be best served by a capacity of about 400. The lower limit would be, say, 250, and the upper limit, 1,000; and these will be the limits taken for granted here unless otherwise specified.

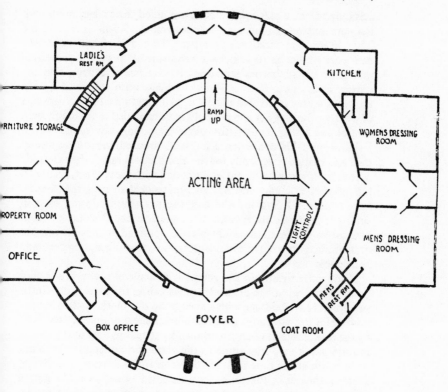

LADIES
REST RM

KITCHEN

FURNITURE STORAGE

WOMENS DRESSING
ROOM

RAMP
UP

ACTING AREA

PROPERTY ROOM

LIGHT CONTROL

MENS DRESSING
ROOM

OFFICE

MENS
REST RM

BOX OFFICE

FOYER

COAT ROOM

4. Plan of the Penthouse Theatre in Washington, Seattle.
It has an elliptical acting area.

Theatre in the round has become a subject of interest during the last dozen years, as one of many so-called new theatre forms. But during this period new plays and new playwrights have in fact dominated both the practical world of the theatre and the discussion that arises from it. Although the opening of Bernard Miles' delightful Mermaid Theatre caused a real stir, and the gallant attempt at a thrust stage at Chichester received a great deal of publicity, there has been little attention paid to the special qualities of these and other theatres with unusual stages by professional men of the theatre, and certainly the new playwrights have not allied themselves at all with the new theatres. In fact two old theatres, the Royal Court and the Theatre Royal at Stratford, have been the homes of so many of the new playwrights as to suggest a reconsideration of the proverbial new wine in old bottles situation. It may be, of course, that the impact of the post-*Saint's Day* writers has been enfeebled by the theatres they have had their plays staged in. It is not simply a question of whether the plays of anger would have exploded more loudly on a central stage than behind the old proscenium, but rather would Osborne and his contemporaries have aroused more response if they had written specifically for the new theatres rather than the old? The new plays can be staged in the round with great effect, certainly, but playwrights, and, indeed, all professional men of the theatre, have to earn a living and the new theatres simply do not exist in sufficient numbers to warrant serious attention. Discussion about new forms of theatre has only been widespread because it touches dramatic activities not just in the profession, but also among amateurs and educationists.

Historically theatre in the round is difficult to place. We cannot point to its beginnings precisely, as we can in the case of the European picture-frame stage which springs up during the Italian renaissance. Nor can we find it ever reaching an ideal of the sort achieved by the open stage in Greece as shown by so many ruins of the fourth century BC, or in Tudor times as the plays of Shakespeare proclaim, or in Spain at the time of Lope de Vega and Calderon de la Barca. Instead, theatre in the round lays claim to being a very primitive form of theatre, probably the common beginning for most formal drama that is known to us. In the Middle Ages it was used in a specially developed form and in modern times it has reappeared, notably in the USA, but also in Europe. Let us look at some aspects of this development in detail, to see what is still relevant.

It is impossible to give a simple factual account of the origins of drama. We do not know the facts. Theatre seems to have existed before writing, before even speech had been achieved. But we may surmise that long ago men felt the need to express themselves, to externalise their feelings about each other and about the world around them, and that they fulfilled this need in dance. Man danced particularly to explore his relationship with the surrounding world, to explain how it behaved, and above all to try and influence its behaviour, to exercise and exert his will power. Man hunted, man farmed; animals were swift or savage, and the rain and the sun made plants grow, blossom, fruit, seed, die and grow again. In a small primitive society, having perceived these things, men were anxious to assure the future—the success of the hunt, the return of spring and fruit-time. Man danced for utilitarian reasons. The dancers took on the roles of prophets and priests, negotiating a desired future from the powers, the gods; they were concerned with bargaining for time, in the future, by offering time, in the present; the ephemeral is to be exchanged for the permanent. They performed in the open air, surrounded more or less informally by their fellows. In so far as this was theatre it was theatre in the round.

The first technical device the dancer used was disguise. Paint, mask, costume. The perennial equipment of the actor. Thus they made more convincing the hunter and the beast, the farmer and the spirit of spring. To help the dance, to increase its power, men made noises. From noise grew music, language, song. And soon language became a particularly powerful weapon in the actor's armoury. As human beings increased their control over their material surroundings and became civilised, their drama took on formal patterns, was assigned to special days and special occasions and special places. Thus, for instance, we find evidence of circular threshing floors used for ritual drama in Greece; and they survived as "theatres", apparently, even at a time of advanced civilisation, when the utility of the dance had been forgotten.

The demand for a theatre structure arose naturally out of the popularity of the drama. When a lot of people gathered together to watch a performance, the circles of spectators could see better if those outside were raised above the people in front of them. Sloping ground would help. But it is difficult to find a natural theatre for a wholly surrounding audience; most hills only partially surround a convenient acting area—simple craters are uncommon and usually unsuitable anyhow. So the great Greek theatres, while retaining the circular acting area, nestled against hillsides that provided only a partially surrounding auditorium.

So far, so much guesswork. We are on firmer ground—though it is not as firm as we might like—in the Middle Ages. There are many books on the medieval drama, and most of those that are written in English refer to the four great cycles of mystery plays—the York, Chester, Coventry and Towneley (or Wakefield) plays. An account of the staging techniques of the York cycle is frequently given. It is generally assumed that each of forty-eight plays of the York cycle was staged on its own pageant wagon. Each wagon was a two-storied erection, the bottom storey being shrouded so that it would serve as a retiring room for the actors, and the upper storey forming the stage. Archdeacon Rogers' well-known description of a pageant car at Chester implies processional performance, and most people assume that this was the common method of staging medieval plays. The pageant cars, numbering as many as there were plays in the day's cycle, were driven through the streets, halting in turn at certain places; and each was used for a performance of a particular play at successive places throughout the day. The organisation of a processional performance of this sort must have been highly complicated and it is hard to understand why it came to be adopted. But, after all, it is an idea based on slender evidence. We have accepted the idea, perhaps, only because we don't have to face the difficulties. The truth is that nothing of the sort need have taken place. If we could find evidence of a simpler alternative, it might prove more likely.

Two helpful notes. Firstly, no matter how firmly the alternative may be established, it does not prove that the processional performance, however difficult, could never have been undertaken; two, or more, methods may have been equally available and used here and there as appropriate. Secondly, it is important to cast doubt on the famous testimony of Archdeacon Rogers. He died in 1595, and is supposed to have witnessed one of the last performances of the Whitsun plays at Chester before they were suppressed. However, the miracle plays had a long run, and many changes of cast and theatre; they probably began to take shape in the twelfth century, and were performed in church by priests. During the four hundred or so years from this beginning, the plays left the church for the open air, recruited their actors from the guilds (and even from professional performers), and the texts were handed on by word of mouth and thus altered, added to, re-edited; and finally written down because the Tudor monarchs imposed a censorship. So the value of Archdeacon Rogers' description is that it gives us information about the last stages of the Chester cycle. Much can happen in several hundred years and what may have been appropriate to the final phase of development need not have been a permanent feature from the start.

Clues to an alternative lie in several places. First, in the *décor simultané* that seems to have been widely used in Europe, and indeed, must surely have been employed when the mystery plays were originally performed in church. Various scaffolds or stages each with its own mansion or scenic house, were laid out fairly close to each other, and actors moved from one to the next when the story demanded a fresh background.

Second, within the plays themselves characters make specific movements from one place to another and it seems likely that in many cases each place may have been a different mansion. For instance, in the Wakefield plays there are a series of scenes connected with the Nativity. Shepherds have a lengthy discussion after which they go to sleep, have a vision of angels, and, after further discussion, they finally travel to Bethlehem and greet Mary. (In the so-called Second Shepherds' Play there is even a visit to a cottage en route.) The three Kings enter separately on horseback, consult with Herod, then go on to greet Mary, and depart, each on his several way. In the next scene Joseph and Mary flee. Then back to Herod. Each of these scenes is indeed confined in scope and in the number of characters, who for the most part, do not carry on from scene to scene. But the manger and Herod's palace are used more than once and it is possible that, here at least, a processional performance could not easily have been managed.

Third, we must look outside the four great mystery cycles, to a fifth. It is a literary Cinderella, seldom given the attention it deserves. The main reason for its neglect is that it is not written in English (nor in Latin) and therefore lies outside the boundaries of English literature. But it was written in England, so no other national literature could be expected to adopt it, particularly as its language is Cornish. Virtually a dead language. However, the cycle is interesting for several reasons. It survives in a text that is probably older than that of its better-known sisters; the scenes are clearly arranged for continuous action, but divided into three parts for three separate days; and, most important of all, there are plans to show how the staging was arranged.

We have half a dozen plans of medieval stages in England. One of them accompanies the manuscript of *The Castle of Perseverance*, and the others come from Cornish plays (including the early sixteenth-century *Meriasek*). These plans all show a similar arrangement; a circular disposition of mansions. How the actors and audience fitted into the plan has been carefully worked out in Richard Southern's book, *The Medieval Theatre in the Round*.* The mansions were used in turn, their scenic character providing a series of specific backgrounds. The audience moved freely from before one mansion to the

* Richard Southern, *The Medieval Theatre in the Round* (Faber & Faber).

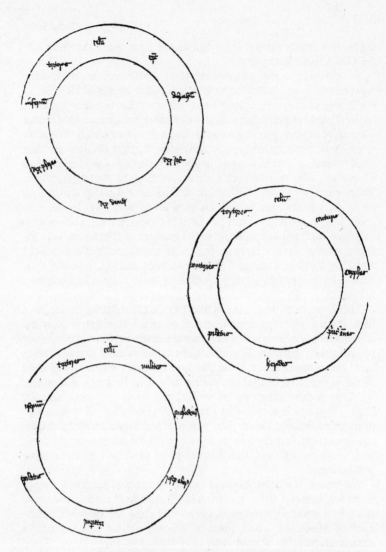

5 (*a*). Three drawings from the medieval MS of the Cornish *Ordinalia*, or mystery plays. The cycle is divided into three parts, played on successive days, and the drawings show the arrangement of peripheral mansions for each day's performance. (*Reproduced by kind permission of the Bodleian Library, Oxford.*) See also the next drawing, and the plates opposite page 87.

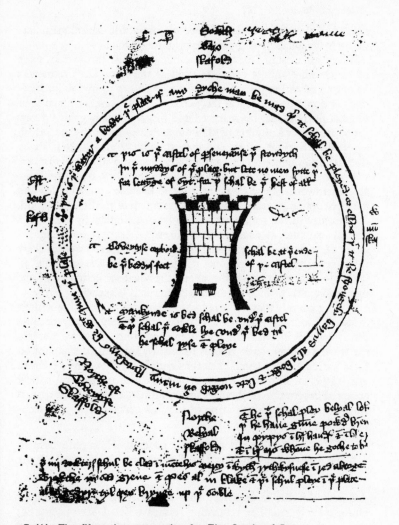

5 (*b*). The fifteenth-century plan for *The Castle of Per-*
severance shows only five peripheral mansions (or scaffolds), but the eight mansions of the Cornish plays are
perhaps implied by the blank spaces. The castle makes the
locale of the central acting specific while in the Cornish
plays it was a general scene of action. (*Reproduced by kind
permission of the Folger Shakespeare Library.*)

next. And the actors made considerable use of the central area, particularly for journeys and scenes of vigorous action.

There still exist in Cornwall a number of circular earthworks, some of which were almost certainly used as theatres. The earthworks belong to an earlier period of history; they were primitive fortifications or domestic enclosures for, perhaps, herding cattle. When their original purpose had been served and forgotten, they gained a new use as arenas for a number of different activities at which the Cornish excelled—wrestling, sports and games, combats and other trials by strength and valour—as well as for plays. Such univallate hill forts are not restricted to Cornwall, and it is likely that they, and other suitable earthworks, were used for athletic exercises, ceremonies and play performances from time to time in much of medieval England.

A theatre in the round could also be made either by building a special structure, as suggested by Carew,* or simply by forming a circle of pageant carts in a market-place. The former seems likely to be restricted to professional companies, while the latter fits in with most of what we know about the amateur activities of the medieval guilds in such towns as Beverley and Wakefield.

It is a great pity that we have to be so cautious in accepting written evidence about early theatres. Caution is necessary if only because the evidence is inconsistent, and often conflicting. When we examine the witnesses, their backgrounds frequently throw further doubt on their testimonies, or sometimes they simply lay themselves open to our suspicion. Having suggested that Archdeacon Rogers' widely accepted description of the pageant performance may not be true, it would be pleasant to subscribe to Carew's version of staging techniques:

> For representing it they raise an earthen Amphitheatre in some open field, having the diameter of his enclosed playne some 40 or 50 foot.

Surely this fits in precisely with the existing Cornish rounds? Unfortunately, no. The remaining rounds which I have measured, some of them mere traces, have diameters nearer 125 ft. Carew goes on to tell an amusing story in mockery of a performance; it gives the impression that he was not sympathetic to theatre. Further, he wrote his Survey at the end of the sixteenth century; and it is fair to ask if he actually witnessed a performance at all. And if he did not, how trustworthy is any of his evidence? In the middle of the eighteenth

* Richard Carew, *Survey of Cornwall* (London, 1602).

1. The Library Theatre in Scarborough.

2. "Circle of Love", the first play presented at the Library
Theatre in 1955.

3. The Penthouse Theatre in Atlanta.

4. The first production at the Pembroke Theatre in Croydon.

century, the antiquary, William Borlase, described in detail two
surviving rounds; but even he cannot always be accepted as a reliable
witness on account of his penchant for finding Druids so frequently
at work. However, these two particular rounds are still the best
among the survivors in the mid-twentieth century and much of what
Borlase put down can be checked. The round at St Just, Penwith
(near Cape Cornwall), has deteriorated considerably since his day;
all one can say is that the diameter of 126 ft is agreeable; it is no
longer an "exact circle", heights are meaningless, and there is little
sign now of seats consisting "of six steps 14 inches wide and 1 foot
high" nor of the possibility that the "benches are of stone".* His
description of Piran round (St Piran's Round) is more consistent
with the present-day state of the earthworks, except that the soil
has obviously slipped and flattened a good deal during the inter-
vening years. All the same, I find it difficult to believe that even in
his day the steps on the inner slope were quite as precise as his
drawing suggests.† This round is often referred to as Perranzabuloe
round: there *is* a round near the village of Perranzabuloe but it has
long been ploughed into the ground and divided by an earth wall and
hedge (from the top of which its shadow can just be perceived and
checked against an ordnance survey map). Perranzabuloe is also the
name of the district and the round is, in fact, a mile and a quarter
east of Perranporth near the hamlet of Rose, and, at the time of
writing, is still worth a visit.

Unfortunately we cannot check other attractive ideas and opinions
put forward by Borlase:

> In these continued rounds or amphitheatres of stone . . . the
> Britons did usually assemble to hear plays acted, to see the
> sports and games, which upon particular occasions were in-
> tended to amuse the people. . . .

> In these same cirques also were performed all their athletary
> exercises, for which the Cornish Britons are still so remarkable;
> and when any single combat was to be fought on foot to decide
> any rivalry of strength or valour, any disputed property or any
> accusation exhibited by martial challenge, no place was thought
> so proper as these enclosed cirques.

I quote the above because I like the proposition that a theatre
should be used for more than mere plays. It is an idea that I will

---

* Borlase, *Antiquities of Cornwall*, 1754.
† Borlase, *Natural History of Cornwall*.

return to. All the same, I doubt if Borlase could have proved his case, and no one now can say positively if he was right or wrong. It is fair, though, to weigh Carew, Borlase and the early scripts of the Cornish plays against Archdeacon Rogers: the evidence for the medieval theatre in the round against processional performance.

It is not unreasonable to suggest that the medieval theatre in the round was indeed very common, and that it lasted in a slowly evolving form right up to Shakespeare's day. Martial Rose, who recently edited the Wakefield cycle of plays, carefully examined the evidence for deciding on the method of staging these plays, as well as the more familiar plays of the York cycle. He concludes:

> The processional street-pageant staging of the York cycle has been too readily accepted without due consideration given to the practical problems involved. . . . There is sufficient evidence to suggest that they [the Wakefield plays] were performed in the mid-fifteenth century at least, when the Wakefield master had written his plays and made so many other revisions in the cycle, in one fixed locality, on a multiple stage, and in the round.*

Staging in the single locality of a theatre in the round does not, of course, rule out the whole idea of procession (surely a most important element in these performances) but simply divorces it from actual performance. The procession might immediately precede performance announcing, early in the day, that the plays were to be performed. Such a procession could be assumed to include the pageant carts, each with its *tableau vivant*—like so many floats in a university rag procession—and as many helpers as possible to bang drums, blow trumpets, and in other ways get the attention of the public and entice them to the market-place or wherever the plays were to be given.

The separate elements of procession and theatre in the round fit in, as well as any other interpretation, with what we know even about the York cycle. In several of the individual plays it is possible to detect where the action leaves the mansion, or pageant, and comes down into the central acting area. For instance, in the *Abraham and Isaac* play Isaac says:

"Children, lead forth our ass. . . ."

and servants come forward precisely for this purpose. The medieval

* Martial Rose, *The Wakefield Mystery Plays* (Evans Bros.).

players surely used a real ass here, and made a real, if abbreviated
journey into the central space among the audience. The dialogue that
follows is perfect coverage for a journey:

I SERVANT	At your bidding we will be bound;
	What way in the world ye will is well.
2 S	Why, shall we truss ought forth o'town,
	To any unknown land to dwell?
I S	I hope thou have in this season
	From God in heaven some solace sent.
2 S	To fulfil it is good reason
	And kindly keep what he has lent.
I S	But what they mean certain
	Have I no knowledge clear.
2 S	It may not greatly gain
	To move of such matter.
ABRAHAM	Annoy you not in no degree
	So for to deem here of our deed.
	As God commanded, so work we:
	Unto his tales we must take heed.
I S	All those that will his servants be,
	Full specially he will them speed.
ISAAC	Children, with all the might in me
	I praise that God of every land,
	And worship him certain;
	My will is ever thereto.
2 S	God give you might and main
	Right here so for to do.
ABRAHAM	Son, if our Lord God almighty
	Of myself would have his offering,
	I would be glad for him to die,
	For all our health hangs in his hand.
ISAAC	Father, forsooth even so would I,
	Liever, than long to live in land.
ABRAHAM	Ah, son, thou sayest full well thereby;
	God give thee grace ready to stand.
	Children, bide ye here still;
	No further shall ye go.
	For yonder I see the hill
	That we shall wend unto.*

* J. S. Purvis, *The York Cycle of Mystery Plays* (SPCK).

It is likely that the hill was in the very centre of the acting area. Abraham's sacrifice anticipates (or certainly did so for medieval people) the Crucifixion which may have been staged in the centre of the theatre also, reflecting its central significance in the religious belief of the audience of those days.

From the earliest times to the present day, all over Europe, Mummers' Plays have been performed in the midst of a circle of spectators. It is a nice irony that the traditional opening line:

"A ring, a ring, I enter in . . ."

has been explained by a stage direction in modern versions, referring to the ringing of a bell, whereas it is itself a kind of stage direction, spoken by the actor in order to get the audience to make a circular space for the action.

The evolution of the medieval theatre in the round and its legacy to the Elizabethan theatres have been carefully traced by F. E. Halliday.* But we usually assume that the Elizabethan public theatre derived from the various relevant elements of the bear-baiting pit with its surrounding galleries and the booth stage introduced into the inn yard. As well as these possibilities, it is worth considering that the medieval theatre in the round developed organically into the Elizabethan public playhouse, firstly by diminishing the number of mansions, retaining for a time just two. Two opposed houses. Heaven and hell-mouth. These may still be discernible perhaps in the houses of Montague and Capulet, and it seems likely that a central acting area, as well as a platform stage, was used even in the Globe theatre of Shakespeare's day. The fencing matches, acrobatics and other entertainments at the Globe took place in the central arena; and the Swan Theatre definitely had a portable stage which could be removed to clear the arena for bear-baiting. The audiences must have been used to action in the middle of these theatres—and why not the action of plays?

For private performances at court a number of mansions were often retained, even so late as for a performance of *Twelfth Night* which Leslie Hotson reconstructs with enthusiasm:

> If the audience was unquestionably *all around*, the actors could certainly be nowhere but in the centre of the room. Shakespeare's production [of *Twelfth Night*] was therefore not against a wall. It was not even against a blackcloth. They [the

* F. E. Halliday, *The Legend of the Rood* (Oxford University Press).

Elizabethans] show us reality; the play being acted openly *out
in the middle of the floor*—an island of drama surrounded by
crowded scaffolds on all sides. A cock-pit. A circus. An arena.
A wooden O. The first performance of *Twelfth Night*, presented
by Shakespeare completely "in the round".*

A small but interesting point is raised by Ben Jonson's title page.
He had it engraved to his own specifications by William Hole in 1616
for the first edition of his collected works. Tragedy balances the
figure of Comedy on each side, and most of it is clear enough. But
one particular panel is baffling. It shows a *visorium*; a circular performing area, with an altar in the middle, surrounded by half a dozen
steeply stepped circular rows. Some dancers are shown, apparently
celebrating a sacrifice that burns on the altar. But why? Where did
Jonson, or Hole, get the idea from? Possibly it is meant to be a
classical Greek theatre; but what gave them the mistaken idea that a
classical Greek theatre looked like this? Certainly not surviving ruins.
What in fact had either of them seen that resembled this, which
might be called a *visorium*, whether or not it was intended to represent a Greek theatre? A likely answer is that Jonson had seen old
provincial theatres in the round in England and had based his concept of a classical or primitive theatre on this homely original.

* Leslie Hotson, *The First Night of Twelfth Night* (Rupert Hart-Davis).

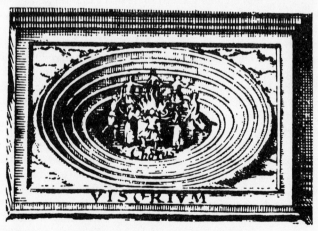

6. Detail from the bottom right-hand corner of Jonson's
title page. (*Reproduced by kind permission of the British
Museum.*)

Accounts of theatre in the round performances occur sporadically in various places at different times, from the Middle Ages to the early twentieth century. It is difficult to explain this widespread hardiness except by assuming that the tradition of central staging has been common and continuous. If more has not been written about it this is because it is so simple a form of theatre. The tradition has been kept alive principally by folk plays and amateur performances that are only occasionally recorded.

In twentieth-century England theatre in the round performances were given by such amateur companies as the Questors Theatre as early as 1926. Among the first pioneers was Peter Slade, whose work in child drama has had a wide influence (and has everywhere been closely associated with informal staging techniques); his first central stage productions date back to 1925, when he was still at school, and subsequently with the Fen Players. Then with various groups in Germany he moved towards a professional theatre company that combined educational work and theatre in the round production, leading to the Pear Tree Players, formed in 1955. The fruit of this work has been enjoyed by young people who have grown up and themselves helped to give a wide ranging interest in theatre to all sorts of people outside the professional theatre. In the amateur field, Jack Mitcheley began in 1948 with the Conesford Players. He has since presented all sorts of plays on central stages as well as many other odd forms of theatre (and conventional theatres too). Brian Way has taken professional companies all over the country, playing in schools and halls, with plays aimed at providing in the broadest sense, an educational stimulus—as well as giving entertainment and fun. Each of these directors has done enough interesting work to justify a book apiece, and I hope such books will soon be written.

The possible continuity of theatre in the round in England is matched by the survival of folk plays in India, performed from time immemorial at crossroads where villagers assemble of an evening and surround the performers. Again, on the seashore near a big town the carpet salesman sets up a complete theatre in the round constructed swiftly with bamboo, in order to display his wares. In India, too, the poet, suddenly inspired, begins his song; the audience gathers round him and, in response to the rapt attention of his listeners, he acts alone the different characters in the story. Performing in this way, the guru depends on the fundamental magic of theatre, more powerful because it calls for no secondary aids. Small wonder that Rabindranath Tagore wrote:

The theatres which have been set up in India today, in imitation of the West, are too elaborate to be brought to the door of all. In them the creative richness of the poet and player is overshadowed by the mechanical wealth of the capitalist. If the Hindu spectator has not been too far infected with the greed for realism; if the Hindu artist has any respect for his own craft and skill, the best thing they can do for themselves is to regain their freedom by making a clean sweep of the costly rubbish that has accumulated and is now clogging the stage.

The Americans, who have often looked west as well as east for their artistic source of materials, have been eager to try out different forms of staging. As early as 1914 an American college began to explore the possibilities of central staging, and in 1947 Margo Jones opened the first professional theatre in the round at Dallas, Texas. There are now many theatres in the round in the United States. Among them the Penthouse Theatre at the University of Washington in Seattle was the first to be built for the purpose. It has an elliptical plan and seats 172 spectators. The Arena Theatre in Washington, DC, is among the newest buildings, has a square acting area, and seats 400 people. The Drury Lane Theatre, in the southern suburbs of Chicago, is under a smart restaurant; there is not enough height to raise seating rows adequately, and the stage is raised about eighteen inches. There is a particularly charming little theatre in the round at Tufts University in Medford, Massachusetts. The Alley Theatre in Houston, Texas, is in a converted warehouse, and the Playhouse in the same city is a specially built theatre in the round with a circular auditorium plan and a revolving stage. The Casa Mañana in Fort Worth, Texas, is again circular and looks magnificent, being housed under one of Buckminster Fuller's geodesic domes. It has a raised stage and differs from those previously mentioned in that it is large, seating 2,000 people. There is an orchestra pit and it is used mainly for musical comedies and light opera. There are many temporary theatres of this size under canvas, with perhaps an excavated auditorium and semi-permanent stage designed, like the Casa Mañana, to present musical shows—usually during the summer.

These theatres vary in size, seating 100 or 2,000 people, and in shape, from circular through oval to rectangular or square. Several of them were built specifically as theatres, others have been converted—from an old warehouse, a gymnasium, a chapel and so on. Several of them make use of a small peripheral stage—a section of seating removed to provide a side acting area.

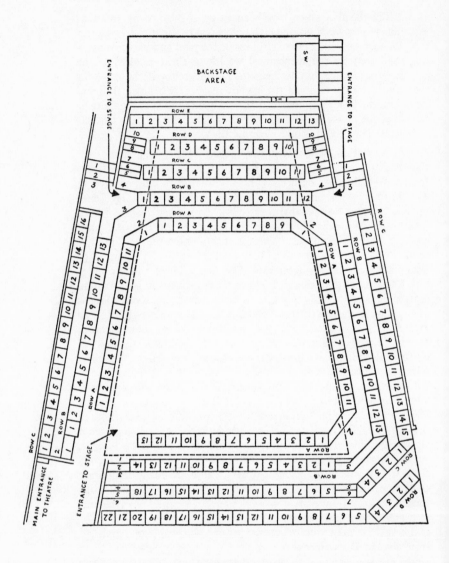

7. In Dallas, Texas, Margo Jones opened the first professional theatre in the round. A conversion of an old building, it had an unusual seating plan.

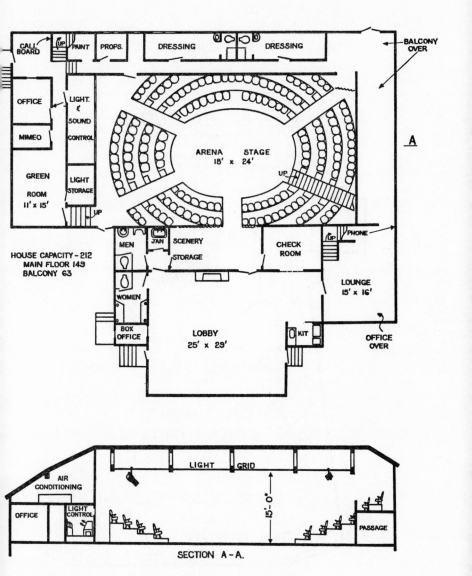

CALL BOARD · UP · PAINT · PROPS. · DRESSING · DRESSING · BALCONY OVER

OFFICE

LIGHT. & SOUND CONTROL

MIMEO

ARENA STAGE
18' x 24'

UP

A

GREEN ROOM
11' x 15'

LIGHT STORAGE

UP

HOUSE CAPACITY - 212
MAIN FLOOR 149
BALCONY 63

MEN · JAN · SCENERY STORAGE

CHECK ROOM

UP · PHONE

WOMEN

LOUNGE
15' x 16'

BOX OFFICE

LOBBY
25' x 29'

KIT

OFFICE OVER

AIR CONDITIONING

LIGHT GRID

OFFICE

LIGHT CONTROL

15' - 0"

PASSAGE

SECTION A-A.

8. Tufts University, Medford, has made a delightful conversion of an old gymnasium into a theatre in the round.

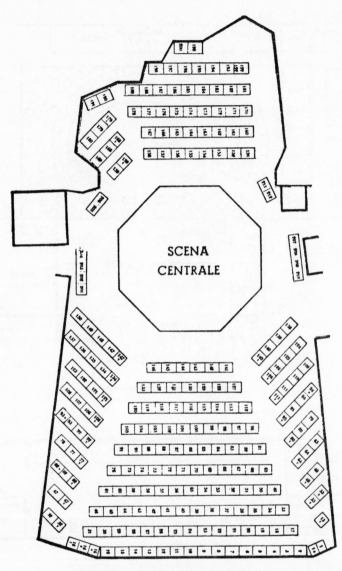

9. *Teatro Sant' Erasmo*, Milan, is asymetrical and might be considered as having a transverse rather than a central stage, as the seating plan shows. The rows of seats are steeply stepped.

In the United States it would not be difficult to find every form of theatre, and many variations of each form. In Europe the traditional picture-frame stage is more common and comparatively few theatres have a central acting area. The *Teatro Sant' Erasmo* in Milan is virtually a theatre in the round, and the *Théâtre en rond* in Paris is a straightforward example, with a circular acting area. Several German theatres have a small house that is adaptable and can be used for theatre in the round as at Gelsenkirchen and Mannheim. But there is a tendency for adaptable theatres to settle down to one particular form, and I know of none in Germany that has either been much used as a theatre in the round or that has ended up in this way.

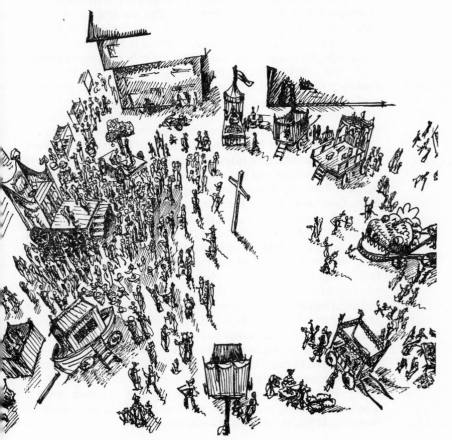

Bird's-eye view of a medieval theatre in the round in the market place.

3
The Studio Theatre Company

In England there have been three professional companies making considerable use of theatre in the round. The first of these opened in Scarborough in 1955 for a summer season, and returned each summer since then until 1965. The second started in 1962 at the Victoria Theatre in Stoke-on-Trent and is now the only permanent theatre in the round in the country. Between 1959 and 1962 the Pembroke theatre flourished in Croydon. Apart from a few brief ventures, professional actors have not otherwise used theatre in the round. The Scarborough and Stoke theatres have both been largely my responsibility and for this reason I have much to say about them.

The main impetus behind the Scarborough theatre in the round was a concern with new plays. This may seem odd now, for playwrights have seldom had less difficulty in getting even passable plays performed than at present. But in 1955 this was not so. The English Stage Company had not yet started, and this company, more than any other, created a revolution in the attitudes of public, managers and critics towards new plays. In 1955 the young playwright seemed to be having a particularly difficult time; not only because managers were unwilling to take risks, but because the widely held and limited concept of what a play should be had a constricting effect on what might even be considered for performance. For several years I had been holding seminars on playwriting, under the aegis of the British Drama League and the Central School of Speech and Drama, and, through these seminars, had become acquainted with several new writers of great promise. Their plays were rejected by enough managements to make me seek a way of staging the plays myself. I had no money of my own, and no one else's was available for a theatre venture based entirely on new plays by unknown writers. The idea of theatre in the round was first considered for reasons of economy. It was the only practicable proposition.

The appeal of theatre in the round, though, was not solely economic. I had seen and enjoyed several theatre in the round performances in the United States. I had for some time been using the idea of a central stage for rehearsing with students and amateurs in order to draw attention to certain basic concepts of acting, and had become fascinated by the possibilities of carrying such exercises further—as far as public performance. But to start my own theatre was a development that I did not then anticipate.

The main hindrance to public performance on a central stage lay in the absence of any properly equipped theatre. The idea of converting a hall could only be carried out if several performances, or a season, were contemplated, so that a budget that included enough money to cover the expense of conversion might be reckoned with; and in the London area I looked at over five hundred halls before concluding that it would be difficult to get a suitable one, at a low rent for a period of several weeks. Meanwhile I talked about theatre in the round to students, to actors and to friends.

In spite of the many theatres in the round in the USA, very few people in this country had then heard of it and many could not even envisage it. Some of my friends, including those whose knowledge of theatre and long experience commanded respect, had no patience with the idea; sometimes because it was new, a gimmick merely, a passing craze; sometimes because it was primitive, a form of theatre no longer valid because we have improved on it. Other people expressed great interest and demanded action. Among those who thought favourably about the idea was J. B. Priestley who, in his book *The Art of the Dramatist*, wrote:

> If I were beginning again, I would move in the opposite direction, towards more elaborate construction and even greater intimacy, taking a few characters through an intricate and ironic dance of relationships. In order to concentrate on ideas, words, subtly intimate acting, I would make a clean break with our picture-frame stage and all its clutter of canvas, paint, carpets and curtains, leaving designers and sets to the movies. I would write for a theatre-in-the-round, the opposite of the movies both in its cost and its art, the theatre where everything visual, except the close and vivid faces and figures of the players, is left to the imagination. For—and I say it for the last time—we cannot have everything at once, and too often when we think we are adding we are subtracting. To pretend about something,

to use the imagination somewhere, heightens and deepens what I have called dramatic experience. And I feel we stand in bitter need of this experience at its best, enlarged, ennobled. As it flashes between those two levels of the mind, often evoking strange and haunting undertones and overtones whispering that all this life of ours may be a shadow show with a deeper reality behind it, I believe it can refresh and even inspire men and women now lost in bewilderment and frustration.*

For several years John Wood, education officer for the North Riding Education Committee, had asked me to take part in weekend courses and summer schools in Yorkshire, and it was on a weekend course in acting at Wrea Head that he challenged me to put theatre in the round to the test of professional performance to the public. I told him of the difficulties in finding a suitable hall, in London. So he took me to see the concert room in the Central Library at Scarborough; and after a friendly and helpful talk with W. H. Smettem, the librarian, our first booking was made.

The concert room was reasonably suitable for conversion into a theatre in the round; in plan nearly square, 40 ft × 50 ft approximately. Perhaps a bit on the small side. Ceiling height about 24 ft, with a good deal of complicated plaster work above a heavy cornice. The room was on the first floor and its main disadvantage was that of its three doors one was an emergency exit leading directly to an outside escape way, and the other two were both in the same wall, 12 ft apart. Thus all the entrances would have to be made from one side of the acting area. Two adjacent rooms were to be made available to us; one for a dressing room (big enough to be simply partitioned off as two rooms) and the other for an exhibition and refreshment room. On the whole, a very good place in which to make experimental first steps.

The Studio Theatre Company was formed, an educational and charitable company for the purpose of presenting new plays. We chose four plays with reasonably small casts and decided to present each play in repertoire for two separate weeks during an eight-week season. We drew up conversion plans using scaffolding and builders' boards to make raised rows that would take the 248 seats already available in the concert room, and obtained an occasional stage play license from the magistrates. There had been doubts about the license. We were warned by several knowledgeable theatre managers

* J. B. Priestley, *The Art of the Dramatist* (Heinemann).

and others with administrative experience that a theatre in the round might not be allowed. It would necessarily contravene the fire regulations. But the Chief Fire Officer and the Chief Constable examined our drawings and production schemes with sympathy. They found no special hazards (and, I suspect, fewer risks to public safety than in most theatres) and gave their approval in court before the licensing magistrates. We got our license.

During rehearsals the whole company worked with enthusiasm, but not without misgivings. Was it sensible to try presenting not only new plays but also a new form of theatre? Why Scarborough? Wouldn't London be more sensible? What special techniques of acting are required for theatre in the round? We endured the sort of set-backs that fall to most small theatre ventures; our leading actress fell ill and had to be replaced in the middle of rehearsal period; half the money that we had budgeted on to launch the season was to have come from someone who, owing to unexpected events, could no longer give it.

We opened in the middle of a splendidly warm July. Scarborough is a holiday town, spreading along two delightful bays, one of which has a promenade flanked by shops, cafes and amusement arcades. There were then half a dozen theatres presenting variety shows and other light entertainments, an open air theatre seating about 7,000 people, a theatre where the York Repertory Company presented a summer season of plays, and a number of good cinemas. With a resident population of about 50,000, Scarborough was already well served with entertainment. To begin with our audiences were thin. Our money soon began to run out. We were saved by the first rainy day when the theatre filled to capacity. At the end of the season we had not lost all our capital, and the directors decided to keep the company going for another season. Economics are important. But we had also had our enthusiasms roused.

And so each year another and another season was planned. But still on a very *ad hoc* basis. No sureness about the future; each season likely to be the last. No financial security, no proper theatrical facilities, considerable competition, dependence on the weather. I believe the quality of work improved and we certainly learned about the central stage. Soon the temporary fit-up began to impose frustrating restrictions on us. The company kept going, thanks to the generous tolerance of the Libraries Committee, thanks to the support of the Arts Council, thanks to the adventurous spirit of so many young artists. Audiences grew steadily, if only because summer is an

unreliable season, landladies don't like holidaymakers cluttering up
the digs and Scarborough is reasonably short of public shelters. And
when you think about it, what an audience! Many of them people
who would not normally be seen inside a theatre, the very people
that Wesker or Littlewood might rejoice to win over; and from all
over the country, people who would go home with an exciting
experience to talk about and who might even develop a taste for
theatre-going.

Some people who have come to the theatre are clearly knowledgeable theatre-goers. Often enough they ask where the stage is? And
may go on to ask what about scenery, and surely, then, the actors
have to turn their backs on the audience? These are serious questions,
and I deal with them seriously. But it is surprising how many people
actually come to the theatre and take the central stage for granted;
among those that do so are, of course, a number who actually live in
Scarborough and come with the same anticipation of pleasure as
supporters of repertory theatres all over the country. Occasionally
extremists come, devotees of theatre in the round who believe it to
be the only valid form of theatre for the twentieth century; on the
other hand, such a one as the lady with whom I had, approximately,
the following conversation in the foyer:

SHE: It says outside that this is a theatre in the round.

ME: Yes, madam, there is a matinee performance going on now.

SHE: What play are you doing?

ME: *Alas, Poor Fred* by James Saunders.

SHE: I've never heard of it.

ME: It's a new play, having its first production here.

SHE: Young man, you are pulling my leg. I read the *Observer*
  and if you were doing a new play I should have been told
  about it.

ME: If you doubt me, come and see the play tonight.

SHE: I know perfectly well that there isn't a theatre in the round in
  this country. Tonight I am going to the cinema.

Exit the pragmatic lady.

The directors of the Studio Theatre Company always tried to
approach theatrical problems from a rational and businesslike point
of view. They tried to understand traditions but did not necessarily
accept them. Following the American example, programmes in
Scarborough were always given away free. Although so small a
theatre cannot expect to pay for the programmes from advertising,
this was a cost willingly budgeted for. And it is interesting to see

that other and bigger theatres have also followed this policy. During the first season all seats were unnumbered and tickets the same price; in subsequent years, though, two ticket prices have been instituted, if only because some people are only satisfied if they are getting the cheaper tickets while others insist on having the more expensive. And it was resolved that refreshments, as good as possible, should be served at virtually cost price, and after the performance. We always wanted there to be an opportunity for the audience to discuss the performance at leisure.

Many Scarborough people are proud that theatre in the round virtually started its career here. From the start the venture had the support of local amateur groups. This extended beyond helping to set up and dismantle the theatre. Front of house help was recruited from volunteers, and prop-hunting, costume-finding and the distribution of publicity material were all aided by voluntary help, under the supervision of Kenneth Boden. Besides helping us he has, as secretary of the local branch of the BDL, organised an amateur theatre in the round festival at Scarborough which looks like becoming an important annual event in the North of England.

At the end of the first season a limited objective had been achieved. No great success; no real proof of either artistic or commercial viability. But acting on a central stage was exciting from every point of view, and there seemed all sorts of opportunities yet to explore. And the directors had already decided to branch out. In the autumn of 1955 we started a Sunday club in London. The secretary, Owen Hale, and production manager, Minos Volonakis, arranged a monthly series of Sunday night performances in the Mahatma Gandhi Memorial Hall at 41 Fitzroy Square. These performances attempted to follow the pattern established before the war by many such clubs whose main objects were to give a try-out to a new or unusual play, to offer leading parts to young actors engaged for small parts in current West End long runs, to enable established actors to play parts outside their familiar range, to introduce new actors to the London stage, to give opportunities to new producers and other artists and technicians; it was taken for granted that theatre managers, critics and keen theatre-goers would come to see the productions. In the end we had to recognise that we were not able to repeat the pre-war pattern; we persevered for a few years in search of a *modus operandi*, which eluded us, before closing the club in 1958.

During its period of operation, the Sunday club had its moments of pleasure and even success, and we learned a great deal. All the artists taking part did so without payment; and their generosity gave the enterprise a sense of purpose. All sorts of ideas were tried out, in acting, writing and production. Theories were put to the test; unexpected discoveries were made. Many members of the club told us of their enjoyment. And in nearly every production something memorable occurred. Obviously it would not be sensible to record all the productions here, but I must recall a few examples of enjoyment.

I have always been scornful of plays in verse by such writers as Eliot and Fry, and I never realised what poetry in the theatre could do, nor what magic can come from lyrical performance, until I saw the extraordinary opening scene of Lorca's *Don Perlimplin and Belissa in the Garden*, played to perfection by Michael Mellinger and Gwen Nelson, who brought on to the stage a lovely humour, a dry pathos and a technical skill that made the words throb with wonder. The smallness of the theatre helped.

In contrast, the terrifying yet wonderful scene in Margaret Turner's *We Are for the Dark*, when the two elderly sisters, trying to deny that old age can bring feebleness, are forced to face the truth; one of them slips and falls but the other has not the strength to help her up; she has the strength, however, to cope with the idle chatter of the landlady in the next room, concealing the event that really preoccupies her. Ann Pichon and Iris Baker played those sisters with a fragile vigour that gave no room for sentimentality and the small theatre, with its lack of proscenium stage conventions, enabled them to balance skilfully between a prosaic realism and an intensely dramatic emotionalism. In the same play Wilfrid Brambell gave a nicely calculated study of a broken old actor, and the part seemed to gain in pathos because it was not presented on the sort of stage the character belonged to.

In Pirandello's *The Man with a Flower in his Mouth* Anthony Jacobs gave a virtuoso performance, using a well-trained and expressive voice to make the play's bitter question have a sharp taste; and one felt the mutual aid of radio and theatre in the round. He was helped by a soft and responsive partner, a performance suggesting the way the world reacts to, yet absorbs, disaster, from Derek Hart, another actor with good microphone technique. Minos Volonakis directed the programme of one act plays by Pirandello; he understood them, helped the actors to make full sense of the plays while exploring every opportunity in each part, and managed the technical facilities of the hall with resourcefulness. We lit three dozen plays without overloading a thirteen amp plug: an electric kettle demands as much.

Derek Hart and Iris Baker played in *The Last of the Wine*. This play, written for radio, was directed on the stage by Roger Jenkins; Robert Bolt's first theatre production. An intelligent and complex story, it ended with the brave matriarchal figure alone, listening to the approaching aeroplane with its atom bomb—a sound we have heard often enough on the stage since. The links between radio and the central stage have been easy to forge.

However, sheer theatrical exuberance does not necessarily get diluted in the round and it would be difficult to beat the hilarious performance of Ralph Nossek with a mouse crawling up his sleeve, in Saroyan's *The Beautiful People*; he had a concentrated look of such utter conviction that the mouse too seemed to come to life. But reality is never enough in the theatre and it is an artist's skill we are admiring when we cry out "That's it to the life!". Gwen Nelson, comic and, of course, convincingly true, played Harmony Blue-blossom deliciously.

There is a tightrope between art and reality that every actor walks in every performance, and the ease and skill he displays give us much of our pleasure. If closeness to truth appeals strongly from the central stage, how do some of the more deliberately artificial dramatic styles come off? An example or two. Richard Pilbrow directed Ernst Toller's *Masses and Man*. The audience was arranged down two long sides of the hall, forming an avenue stage with the glass entry doors at one end and the platform at the other. He laid on a special electricity main and lit the production with great care. Entrance of the mob, through the glass doors, led by a man racing to the platform with a huge red banner, catching shafts of light. Again, a huddle of people around the platform, machine-gun noises in the distance, sudden darkness, chaos, silence; then a light outside the glass doors (a searchlight, no less) shining in past the figure of a gauleiter in the doorway and throwing his shadow right along the floor to the platform. An expressionistic play with an unexpected punch. Again, Clifford Williams directed his own *The Disguises of Arlecchino*, a pastiche based on the *commedia dell'arte*, and Peter Bridgmont played Arlecchino, entering with a good stage trip, a breathtaking fall flat on his face, and executing the mime and verbal acrobatics with an impudent gaiety, and consummate skill.

We liked one-act plays, and thought that television might take to them. We were wrong. But performances of plays by Adamov and

Tardieu gave us a stimulating introduction to what later came to be known as theatre of the absurd, but which was then, in an article by Irving Wardle in *Encore*, christened the comedy of menace.

Although the Mahatma Gandhi hall had a platform, with a proscenium arch and good curtains, it was not a stage for actors, there being no wing space, overhead space or any other working space; one small dressing room, so we used the platform itself as a dressing room. The hall had been well designed in a modern and lively style; asymmetrical, it had a useful balcony round one and a half sides which provided a lighting gallery as well as a good seating row. It made a very pleasant theatre in the round. The hall served the Indian YMCA, and the residents lent the proceedings a pleasantly exotic air; we were always warmly welcomed, and dress rehearsals usually gained from being interrupted by good curry lunches. After each performance the refectory was thrown open for coffee, a thoroughly successful way to round off the evening; nearly always packed with noisy people, arguing about the play, discussing the performance, comparing opinions, meeting friends, these refreshment sessions often lasted longer than the performances.

The activities of the Sunday club made a steady loss and subsidies were not available for this sort of work. The productions each cost about twenty-five or thirty pounds and ticket sales brought in about fifteen or twenty, leaving us with a deficit of about ten pounds on each performance. The directors, none of them rich, paid out for as long as possible. But in the end we simply could not go on because the Sunday club was clearly not serving the purposes intended. Few well-known actors were interested in performing for us. Few managers or critics came to see the new plays or the young artists (and those that did were often very unimpressed). And an important new consideration was the growing scope of the company's touring schedule, about which I shall say something presently.

The final productions for the Sunday club were carefully chosen. We obtained a license to open the theatre to the public so that each play could be run for two weeks. The first of these productions was David Campton's *The Lunatic View*, a nice example of comedy of menace, that anticipated much of what we were later to see of Ionesco, Pinter and N. F. Simpson. The second production had a distinguished cast, headed by Margaret Rawlings; the play, a translation of Racine's *Phèdre*, had not been previously performed in this country by professional actors in English. The translation most readily available contained lines such as "Urging the rapid car along the strand", and these had to be altered. Miss Rawlings, herself a French scholar, made the adaptation, or, as it soon became, her own complete translation, which was subsequently published.* Each of these productions was then taken out on tour; and the Sunday club ceased its activities.

The Lunatic View was among the most interesting presentations of the Studio Theatre Company. In fact it is not one play, but four short plays, linked together by a particular attitude displayed by the author to his material. In each play the characters travel blindly towards or away from a disaster. One feels the urge to make them open their eyes, to shout at them: "But don't you see?" They are like us, though, and concentrate their energies on loving or hating the superficial things in front of them. And in one play, the author, among other things, demanded no scenery whatever. No props either. The play *Memento Mori* (a title used later for a novel and a play—David Campton has a knack of anticipation) therefore became a special favourite for theatre in the round performance, since only on the central stage could it both be given without a setting and at the same time raise no question of background. A subtle point, perhaps, but one that has wide implications. In another of the plays, set after the explosion of an atom bomb, there are two survivors with their heads in brown paper bags. The idea gave us the opportunity of checking the reactions of people who criticise theatre in the round because they cannot always see the actors' faces. And this play also became a favourite. The remaining two plays became increasingly interesting: with one, *Getting and Spending*, the author had hit upon more than a few similarities with a later and better known play, *The Chairs*; and with the other, *A Smell of Burning*, had anticipated briefly some of the details as well as the general feeling of *The Fire Raisers*. At the time of their first performance the plays that make up *The Lunatic View* seemed to us to be outstandingly original and David Campton's blend of fun and seriousness promised to be very attractive to audiences. Half a dozen years later they are still frequently performed by student and amateur societies.

The production of *Phèdre* grew out of small beginnings. First staged as a Sunday club performance, with a cast of experienced and well-known actors, it was so successful that it was repeated, then cast again (since several of the original company were already working in the West End) and performed in London and on tour. Margaret Rawlings gave an outstanding performance. She brought to the part

* Margaret Rawlings, *Racine's Phèdre* (Faber & Faber).

a rich, wide-ranging voice, great sensitivity and tremendous power. She had all the dignity expected of a queen, together with the ferocious passion that the character demands. But the unexpected touch that brought distinction to her performance was the convincing humanity of it; the audience's sympathy could here be immediately engaged in a play that runs the risk of being very remote. She also worked enthusiastically on her edition of the script; and quietly, unobtrusively, she began to take an interest in the little company that had plucked up courage to present this great play. Then and later she helped the company in the most practical ways possible, and has earned our gratitude and affection.

Phèdre, directed by Campbell Allen, also benefited from the good work of an outstanding young actor, Keith Baxter, who played Hippolytus. In a small theatre the audience can usually sense precisely what is going on in an actor's mind, and when, as in theatre in the round, there are few technical tricks with which an actor can dazzle the public, his concentration and imagination are astonishingly exposed. On this score Keith Baxter gave a deeply moving performance. Of course the part is a fine one, but even a tiny part can be distinguished by a performer who has these powers of concentration and imagination. In *Phèdre* the insignificant part of Ismène, confidante of Aricia, was raised to a character of great beauty by the performance of Constance Lorne. The confidante in a classical French tragedy usually has to do a lot of listening—and not much else. On a central stage, when the heroine is holding forth for dozens of couplets at a time, half the audience is watching the confidante, and in this instance, getting the full impact of the scene from her. Constance Lorne gave a totally unselfish performance but filled the part with a complete and charming personality, a person who somehow reflected (as a confidante should) all the thoughts and emotions of her companion.

I have now seen a very large number of performances on the central stage, and some have been more enjoyable than others; and I find difficulty in agreeing with most of the generalisations that people often give after seeing one or even a few productions. Such generalisations are freely made in print; and we heard them frequently when the company went on tour to places where no one could be expected to have seen much theatre in the round nor, often enough, much theatre of any sort. I find it particularly hard to generalise about the varied performances at the Mahatma Gandhi Hall.

If I admit that the Sunday club performances in London were not well attended on the whole, I must say also that I think they provided us with no conclusive test. How many other Sunday clubs and little theatres have fought a losing battle in post-war London? Enough to permit me to hold on to an increasing certainty that there was more in theatre in the round than I had at first supposed. The people who did come, and the people who visited our summer theatre, seemed to enjoy themselves, and so did the many actors who took part in the productions. And with every production we were learning more and getting more deeply interested in theatre in the round. For these reasons more work seemed justified.

4
Touring and Settling Down

THE Studio Theatre company made its first steps towards touring in a strange way. During our first summer season we received a call for help from a nearby holiday camp. They had booked a small circus to give an afternoon's entertainment; but the circus had cried off; would we go instead? I pointed out that round or not our plays were no substitute for a circus and would probably have little appeal to a holiday-camp crowd. Never mind, this was an emergency, said Mr Wallis, and besides the entertainment was only an insurance against rain. If the weather were fine no one would come anyhow. So we agreed. The dance hall had a convenient dipped area in the middle and by careful arrangement of seating a reasonably satisfactory theatre in the round could be constructed without the use of any rostrums. We presented our current production, *Turn Right at the Crossroads*, an allegorical satire on contemporary society written in modern blank verse. Good, spikey stuff. Morris Perry played the hero, a full length modern Everyman. In rehearsals he had found that he could hardly manage the long speeches, and I recommended him to go into training like an athlete. He did, going for an early morning run throughout the season. The holiday-camp audience appreciated his physical skill if not all else. The play suffered from a diffuse construction and several scenes did not work well in our production. During the first of the weak scenes members of the audience started talking; standing at the back of the hall I could soon no longer hear the actors at all. The disaster we deserved, for taking a highbrow play to a lowbrow audience, seemed imminent. The thing would simply have to come to a stop. But the actors persevered into the next scene—an exciting one—and the audience swiftly grew quiet. Attention became completely concentrated on the performance. The noise grew again for each weak scene, and dropped as soon as the actors and the playwright really deserved attention. This audi-

ence knew by instinct how to criticise a play, and though their
criticism may have been expressed crudely, it was surely honest and
completely sensible; much more compelling than indifference or the
divergent opinions of expert dramatic critics. In the end the play
received an ovation and the actors, thoroughly exhausted, knew they
had given real pleasure to a good audience.

Mr Wallis commented sensibly and kindly on the performance,
and, though we both agreed that our plays were not ideal for the
occasion, he asked us to present, each week, our other plays. And
again next season. I suspect he did this partly out of gratitude; we
had come to his rescue, and he could see clearly enough that we
enjoyed the experience.

The company acted David Campton's farce *Dragons are Dangerous*
at the holiday camp. Like any good farce it began with a ludicrous
scene. Enter an elderly woman in wellington boots, with an umbrella.
She goes to the french windows, screams and dashes from the room
protecting herself with the umbrella. This scene had an extraordinary
effect on a lady in the front row. She was obviously Grandma in a
family group and she laughed a great gurgling toothless laugh, rocked
backwards and forwards and clapped her hands with delight. The
rest of the audience was infected, and from then onwards every character on making an exit (and there were very many) was heartily
applauded. A spontaneous, unique gesture. During the same performance a little boy left his family and wandered round to the
opposite side of the acting area. His progress could be followed by
everyone on account of his little lead boots (as it seemed). Finally, he
looked across at his parents, and suddenly said in a clear voice:
"Mum, can I have a pee?" The little lead boots trotted away to the
back of the hall. No one was the least disturbed by this interruption
and it damaged the performance not a jot.

The Glass Menagerie begins with a soliloquy by Tom; a quiet
piece of retrospection. Our holiday-camp audience talked loudly
throughout this, and the actor, Malcolm Rogers, came off the stage
in despair. But the play began to interest many people and the scene
with the gentleman caller claimed complete silence. This is the best
scene in the play, isn't it? Our audience needed no dramatic critic
to guide them. They responded with remarkable acumen.

However, the holiday-camp performances really were inappropriate and we gave them up after two seasons. With many lessons
gratefully learned, but with a nagging sense of failure. Why were our
performances inappropriate to that audience? Not simply because

of the plays nor of the centre stage; I can think of companies that would have been rejected sooner. The question is big, and not simply related to theatre in the round. But we had learned how easy it could be to move the company from one place to another.

In 1956 we acquired, with the help of the Pilgrim Trust, a carefully designed set of folding rostrums that enabled us to convert almost any hall into a theatre in the round. We now formed a touring company. The rostrums were transported on a three-ton lorry. Props, costumes, spotlights and so on were carried in another lorry. We directed our attention primarily towards otherwise theatreless towns, in the hope that there might be a chance of taking root and finding a home where a permanent theatre could be established. The Arts Council helped by giving grants and by advising on likely places to visit. As the touring schedule got going it was linked to the Scarborough summer season and we were able to tour a repertoire of several plays, each of which had been thoroughly rehearsed. The company played in Leicester (then without any professional theatre), Southampton, Hemel Hempstead, Harlow, Birmingham, Newcastle-under-Lyme, Dartington Hall and Hull as well as in London and Scarborough.

The vehicles had substantial personalities. Our first touring manager, Rodney Wood, had gone with me to various auctions in search of something cheap and reliable. We ended up with one-time British Road Services lorries. One, a flat backed truck, fitted with our specially designed side supports, carried the rostrums. It started easily, made a great noise as though the pistons were for ever clapping their hands, and boiled over if driven at more than twenty-eight miles an hour when loaded. I drove it unloaded with the speedometer reaching the sixty miles an hour mark; this meant a speed of about forty. And it didn't complain. It was coloured red. The other lorry had an enclosed back and we fitted a luton front on it; this was pre-fabricated and put on in a hurry, and, although we resolved to secure it properly one day, it never gave any trouble. We painted this vehicle green. It was slow to start, but steady and not given to steaming like the red vehicle. Both lorries consumed large quantities of oil but were otherwise pleasant enough to drive when you were in the mood. But when, after several weeks in one place, we looked at our lorries they hardly seemed capable of further work; bruised, old and a bit lop-sided, each of them seemed to be crying out to be pensioned off. And every move started with anxiety. However, once the vehicles were loaded and had taken the first few miles in their stride, confidence returned. Rodney was an experienced driver who knew how to cope with situations such as a jammed starter motor, a fit of backfiring (the red lorry of course), or the sudden appearance of a downhill gradient of 1 in 6. In fact the only serious breakdowns occurred, fortunately, when we had time to spare. After one tour the green lorry had to be driven from London back to its garage in Scarborough; half way along the A1, while travelling slowly in a queue of traffic on a one-way stretch, the radiator suddenly blew up. If it had never steamed before the reason now was apparent, it couldn't: the escape route had been blocked. The resulting mess delayed us twenty-four hours. The incident would have been disastrous on tour.

The vehicles were garaged in Scarborough with County Garages, who took an avuncular interest in them. Whenever we wanted them they were ready for us, topped up, tightened up, tested and ready for the road. We were grateful for such help, but a bit disturbed that no one would reassure us about the future. The piston slap on the red lorry caused long faces and predictions of a short period before a new engine became necessary. But no money was available for a new engine.

Our touring routine was strenuous. After a Saturday-night performance the theatre would be taken to pieces; that is to say all the rostrum units and stage lighting were dismantled and loaded on to the lorries. The stage manager took charge of this operation, assisted by the small technical staff of the company and half a dozen volunteers —local amateur actors (always enthusiastic friends) often enough, or schoolboys. As soon as loading had been completed, usually just after midnight, we set off for the next town on our schedule. We travelled overnight because the roads were emptier and because if the vehicles broke down the delay need not prevent our opening in time. As soon as we arrived at our destination, where volunteer helpers would be waiting, the rostrums and lighting equipment would be set up. By tea-time, with another theatre in the round ready for occupation, everyone wanted nothing more than a good sleep. On Monday afternoon the company rehearsed the play to open that evening.

We usually opened with the play that had been performed at the end of the previous visit. In this way we stumbled on an interesting observation of people's critical faculties. Attendances at performances tended to improve during a visit and we often opened to poor houses and ended up playing to capacity. In each town, knowledgeable people assured us we had chosen the wrong play to open with. But presenting four plays in four weeks in four different places meant that each of the plays opened the season in turn. And the most popular play in one town turned out to be the least successful in the next. Always it is easy to be wise after the event, and the whole theatre business is rich with imponderables that should be simple enough to solve, but we never discovered the ideal play to open with.

Our visits to Southampton were made particularly pleasant by our landlord. The hall converted into a theatre in the round belonged to St Mary's Parish Church, and the vicar, the Reverend Roy Chamberlain, and his wife both took a keen interest in what we were doing. They were refreshingly objective about the theatre and helped us with sympathy and intelligence, but without the hearty but limited enthusiasm so familiar among theatre people. The snag about this hall was that the theatre had to be taken down to make room for a regular whist drive each Monday. The whist drive brought in the money—and, indirectly, subsidised even our visits. During one of our matinee performances, a clergyman walked right through the hall, past the actors, and announced in the foyer that some people were rehearsing in the dark.

In Hemel Hempstead the dressing room had to be shared with a baby clinic. There was often fierce competition for space, and orange juice got featured on the make-up tables. Everyone, though, was cheerfully tolerant, and our several visits were always enjoyable. There seemed to be something very right in bringing a new form of theatre to a new town. Indeed, for a time it seemed likely that either Hemel Hempstead or Harlow might actually build a theatre in the round. But for such a large-scale venture, even a new town must in the end accept the more common tradition of a picture frame stage. And our plans never got very far.

Birmingham, which has several flourishing theatres, was put on our touring schedule because the Corporation had recently converted old premises into a small adaptable theatre. We undertook to show how it could be used for theatre in the round. One of the plays we first presented there had an interesting background. Written by a young man I had known when he was a student at the Central School, it had been performed at the Lyric Theatre, in Hammersmith, and, though provoking interested notices, it had been withdrawn after five days. The play baffled me, but it also attracted me strongly and I asked the author to produce it for us. He agreed.

And the company embarked on a fascinating production of *The Birthday Party*, directed by Harold Pinter. The actors enjoyed working with him. He knew precisely how they felt about the play, and precisely how to help them. He seldom tried to explain "obscurities", but instead showed the actors how to do the action, thus giving even the most baffling parts of the play a conviction and organic logic of their own. It played to very thin houses in Birmingham, aroused some protest in Leicester and was instrumental in getting television companies interested in the author. The opening scene was later presented at a charity midnight performance in Scarborough, where, sandwiched between variety acts it was completely successful.

Quite the pleasantest place the company visited was Dartington Hall. The countryside came as a marvellous relief after so much work in towns, more or less ugly. The dance theatre at Dartington became our theatre in the round. It had an altogether friendly and appropriate atmosphere. People came to the theatre from a wide neighbourhood, and brought with them keen expectation, a willingness to enjoy the plays together with a capacity for criticism and vigorous discussion. We enjoyed playing to such appreciative audiences. The place reflected the characters of its owners, Leonard and Dorothy Elmhirst, who had introduced so many fresh and refreshing ideas into all the various activities at Dartington Hall, and who now welcomed us generously.

The touring schedule grew so that in 1960 the company worked for nearly a full year. This meant that many actors stayed with the company for more than one season and benefited from the continuous experience. New actors gained from the experience of others. The tours also had their own attraction. All over the country people had read about theatre in the round and other new forms of theatre, and seized the opportunity to see what it meant in action. In 1960 we received a generous donation from the Gulbenkian Foundation to help improve the scope and standard of our schedule and productions. We were now able to rehearse for three weeks or more, to add another actor to the company, and to improve advertising and public relations.

Rodney Wood, now married, left the company to settle down and raise a family—with a job that brought in a higher salary than we could offer (and, I guess, with working hours more reasonable than ours).

A small theatre company such as ours could not be expected to pay high salaries. But precisely how low they have been, few people realise. Much publicity is given to the fantastic salaries of film stars and top entertainers. A rich impression is liable to rub off on to all actors. Our policy was to give everyone the same wages. Ten pounds a week. No overtime pay, but plenty of overtime work. Travelling expenses paid, but virtually no other privileges or perks. The only actors who got less than this were complete beginners, taken on as students, and we seldom accepted such beginners because every member of the small company had to undertake a full burden of responsibility. The only people to get more were married actors, who were paid £15, unless both husband and wife worked for the company—often a happier alternative. Not only have many people taken it for granted that our salaries have been high, but an even larger number have taken it for granted that an actor's life is an easy one; after all, he only does a few hours work each evening. These misunderstandings arise, of course, to face all small theatre companies. The central stage makes no difference here. But we often resented the airy expressions of envy we met for our easy-going lives.

Rodney left, and Joan Macalpine took over his job as touring manager. She got the appointment partly because she wanted to write plays, and partly because she could drive. Would-be playwrights are two a penny, but Joan could drive the green lorry. While with the company she wrote a delightful adaptation of *David Copperfield*, and a pleasant farce called *A Thief In Time*. She also introduced some system into our correspondence files, mailing lists, and script-reading rotas. Joan seemed to depend on hard work, and the touring company thrived. But it was very hard work, and, in several of the places we visited regularly, much time was spent discussing with local authorities the possibility of a permanent theatre in the round. At first we thought of such a theatre primarily as a base for the touring company. But it soon became an end in itself, a resting place, free from nightmare journeys in unlikely vehicles at awful hours of the night.

Proposals for a permanent theatre in the round had been discussed for several years in Scarborough, but it seemed unlikely in a town where the main industry was entertainment that anything approaching civic support could ever be given to a theatre. Various improvements were made to the concert room so that it could more readily serve our purpose. But the concert room did not belong to us, and we could hardly expect it ever to be more than a makeshift theatre.

In 1961, Arnold Wesker organised the second Trade Union
festival at Wellingborough and asked the company to bring three of
David Campton's one-act plays. The hall we played in had a bus stop
immediately outside and the set-up went swiftly: as buses arrived
ahead of schedule, the crew gave a quick helping hand, until the
next bus arrived, and then set off again a few moments late. The
plays suited the occasion well enough, but for various reasons did not
attract anything other than a typical theatre audience. The busmen
helped set up but did not come to the performances. It is no easy
matter to attract a fresh audience. Most playhouses are filled by a
fairly limited section of the community; characterise them (a bit
brutally) as middle class, middle aged, middle brow and predomi-
nantly female. A small proportion of the population. Put on plays
that might attract younger people and, generally speaking, the
middle-aged ones stay away but the youngsters do not come in
sufficient numbers to justify the performance. So with a policy that
seeks an artisan audience, or an intellectual audience, or a masculine
audience or even, perhaps more sensibly, a wider audience altogether. Still, the nice ladies or nothing. At the Wellingborough
Festival, only the theatre suffered in this way. Poetry in pubs,
abstract art, guitar recitals, oratorios even, won wide attention. But
the theatre. . . . It has a solid reputation.

The performance at Wellingborough was immediately followed
by a special demonstration at the London Welsh Association hall for
the benefit of a Townswomen's Guild Conference. During the conference I gave a talk to the delegates in St Pancras Town Hall,
explaining to them what theatre in the round was, how it fitted into
the history of the theatre, and what use it might be to a townswomen's guild. The talk must have been delivered with fervour.
It had a noisy reception, not entirely sympathetic. A lady leaving the
hall said to her companions, "The man's mad, quite mad."

The officers of the Townswomen's Guilds are kind people and
good organisers. It had been agreed that there should be three
demonstration performances, in order to give all the delegates a
chance of attending; at 1 pm, 5 pm and 8 pm. Each performance
was packed to overflowing. All ladies, mostly middle class and
verging towards middle age. The essence of theatre audience. The
demonstration consisted of a one-act play performed for all it was
worth; then a rehearsal in which the actors and I worked on a short
scene, and finally a first rehearsal with on-the-spot volunteers from
the audience. The one-act play, chosen carefully for the occasion,

consisted of a duologue between two women, discovered knitting on a mountain top. When the time came to start the first run, it was necessary to have good ladies on the door to stop other good ladies from coming in (with the next showing's tickets); the houselights went out on time—but no actors arrived on stage. After a few moments of waiting, the stage manager realised that the commotion at the entrance to the hall was being caused by the two actresses trying to get past the ladies at the door who wouldn't listen to a word of excuse. . . . Otherwise the demonstration went through smoothly enough. The play, *We've Minds of Our Own* by William Norfolk, gave Patricia England and Hazel Burt amusing caricature parts that they played with relish. Dressed in good, solid but slightly shabby suits, dowdy hats and weighty shoes, they knitted away and nattered away to great effect.

Actors could scarcely get more varied audiences than those at Scarborough, at the holiday camp, at Dartington Hall, and at such a demonstration as to the TWGs. We enjoyed the experiences and, I hope, we learned from them some of the important lessons in the general business of entertainment, and the particular business of the central stage.

Our visits to the Municipal Hall in Newcastle-under-Lyme carried a real hope from the start that a permanent theatre might be established here. There had once been a flourishing Georgian theatre that had closed when the larger Victorian theatres opened in the neighbouring Potteries towns. The building had been converted into a cinema and now stood empty, dilapidated and virtually unusable. No one planning a permanent theatre (in the round or any other sort) could fail to note that even the theatres that had replaced the old Royal were now themselves either cinemas or empty shells. The only remaining professional playhouse in the area was the Theatre Royal in Hanley, which had been rebuilt in 1956 after a fire. Its re-opening had been an opportunity for much celebration and it was even called the finest theatre in the provinces. It ceased to be a playhouse in 1962 and turned over to the current craze for bingo. Permanence in the theatre is an elastic concept.

In Newcastle we had the help and advice of Charles Lister, the Borough Treasurer, who himself wanted to see a civic theatre established. He looked at our accounts with great care, came to see every play, and discussed with us all the important financial, artistic and social implications of theatre. In 1962 the final proposals for a civic theatre gained the support of a majority in the council chamber.

5. "Little Brother, Little Sister" presented at Centre 42's Wellingborough Festival. (*Photo Roger Mayne.*)

6. "We've Minds of our Own", a demonstration performance to Townswomen's Guilds at the Welsh Institute in London.

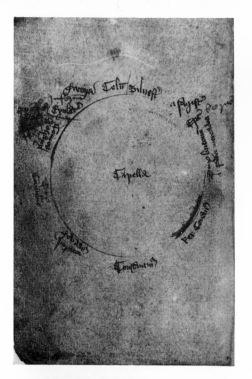

7 and 8. Together with the drawings on pages 20 and 21 these sketches show the arrangements for staging medieval Cornish plays. The upper drawing is particularly interesting because it shows that a structure was erected in the middle of the acting area, as in "The Castle of Perseverance". Both these drawings are stage plans in the manuscript of the Cornish saint's play, "The Life of St Meriasek". (*Reproduced by kind permission of the National Library of Wales.*)

But the plans collapsed at last against an unexpected obstacle put in their way by the Minister of Housing and Local Government. In technical terms, loan sanction was refused. But by the time the fatal blow was delivered, we had already undertaken to establish a company in temporary premises so that an audience could be built up and a policy established by trial and error for the new theatre. Ironically, too, the premises we finally found were just over the border that separates Newcastle from Stoke. For Charles Lister this must have added insult to injury. But our audience had to come from a wide area and the theatre would have to serve the whole of the Potteries, indeed the whole of North Staffordshire, and from this point of view the position carried no disadvantages.

The Victoria Theatre had been built as a small cinema, serving an artisan residential locality, on the main road between Stoke and New-castle. The site unfortunately included no car parking facilities, and the frontage could never be anything but modest. But in many ways the building itself seemed ideal for conversion. Several plans were drawn up. We had only a few pounds available and a few promises. At worst we could simply clear away the debris and set up our port-able rostrum units as soon as the Scarborough season had finished. But generous help came from William Elmhirst and Miss Margaret Rawlings; Granada Television offered us surplus seating from their cinemas; ABC Television presented us with a cheque for £700; and the Gulbenkian Foundation paid for much-needed decoration in the foyer. We were able to embark on a fairly substantial scheme of alterations. Our architect, Peter Fisher, took full charge of the con-version while the summer season kept us at Scarborough. He drew up plans for permanent seating rows, the construction of dressing rooms, an extensive control room and arrangements to put at any rate some spotlights in the roof void. The work had to be carefully discussed and detailed if it were to be completed in time for the Scarborough company to move in. Experienced theatre people whose advice we sought were mostly discouraging. And the familiar arguments that no theatre could succeed in the Potteries were re-inforced by the unlikeliness of the place. And we were told authorita-tively that the conversion plans could not be completed in the time available. Fortunately everything went smoothly enough.

The Victoria Theatre opened on 9 October 1962 with a per-formance of *The Birds and the Wellwishers*, a play by William Norfolk that had been among the new productions at Scarborough. Directed by Peter Cheeseman, the play gave good comic opportunities to

C

Alan Ayckbourn as an earnest do-it-yourself clerk and to an adenoidal Elizabeth Bell as a romantically minded telephonist. The author had written the play with a fine sense of humour that appealed strongly to young people. In some ways it was a good play to open with. Thoroughly entertaining, well acted, unconventional. It attracted people with bright minds, or with a simple desire to enjoy themselves. It did not attract people looking for secondhand West End successes, nor the dramatic critics who were invited and, for reasons unknown, did not come. Was it the new play or the new theatre that kept them away? The following plays included Pinter's *The Caretaker* and David Campton's adaptation, from Poe, of *Usher*. These plays established the fact that the Victoria Theatre had decided to look for a young audience or an audience of any age that did not have too stereotyped a notion of what a play should be.

Peter Cheeseman assumed the job of manager, in charge of the Victoria Theatre, with a free hand and the responsibility to get the thing going. No easy task. If in an area as highly populated as the Potteries there is no theatre and if, further, a few years ago there used to be several theatres, it is not a rash conclusion that the people don't want a theatre and know they don't want one. Obviously the situation is not as simple as that. Perhaps the theatres were too big, or had the wrong policy, or were in one way or another out of date or otherwise unsuitable. But the Victoria Theatre, no matter how much it tried to avoid mistakes could not escape the disadvantages of its situation, its lack of car-parking facilities, the sheer simplicity (to use a polite word) of its conversion, and above all the known fact that a theatre is not for the likes of us (as it were). But Cheeseman set about the task of winning an audience with huge enthusiasm and bristling energy. Results so far: a young audience, growing attendance figures and some interesting successes—notably Marlowe's *The Jew of Malta*, Brian Way's *Pinocchio* and the theatre's own musical entertainment called *The Jolly Potters*.

In *The Jew of Malta* Bernard Gallagher gave a surprising performance. His Jew had not only the cynical mockery obvious enough in the part, but also a substantial sense of humour that is less often perceived in Marlowe's character. In fact, of course, Marlowe is too often denied a humorous gift because the humour is, perhaps, difficult to notice in a reading: it is not in the words so much as in the events. But it is easy to see in performance when an actor of this power and integrity gets to grips with such a role as the Jew.

Gallagher showed the two qualities of humour and integrity to quite different effect in de Hartog's play *The Fourposter*. Again it is often said that this play is trivial, but here the actor brought before us a genuine picture of a delightful man in the process of growing wise; and there is nothing trivial about that. He was partnered in *The Fourposter* by Elizabeth Bell; she gave the part a warm humanity that gripped the attention of the audience. A young actress of wide ranging talent; splendid as the bloody heroine in *Usher*, creating an entirely original character of deep seriousness with hysterically funny effect in *The Birds and the Wellwishers*, and playing with a mature and crisp style in Anouilh's *The Rehearsal*.

Alan Ayckbourn's play, *Standing Room Only*, had a second production at the Victoria Theatre, which prompted him to write yet another play, *Mr Whatnot*, this time paying special attention not only to the various talents of the actors but also to some of the particular opportunities in the Victoria Theatre. The story deals with a piano tuner, who is dumb and who pursues the beautiful daughter (dumb in a metaphorical sense) of an aristocratic family. At this level the play had just enough substance to provide a beginning, middle and end. But it was written for performance without scenery and changed scene frequently, including several journeys—across acres of garden, down dark passages and even in speedy vehicles along the highway. Real properties, phoney properties and mime properties all enriched the scene, ranging from a genuine steering wheel to represent a car, to an entirely imagined piano that was played furiously. Here actors found unending opportunities for creating the substance of reality from the merest hint of its existence. The stuff of drama. Finally, the chaos caused by the dumb man, played by Peter King, an impossible clown enlightened by absolute good sense, in the complete family, symbol of a stable society, caused the audience to feel an exhilaration as though they had had a glimpse of a new freedom. The play made a pointing gesture in the direction of anarchy, and the acting, too, showed what vitality and joy can come from the efforts, freely contributed, individually chosen, and carefully selected, of individual artists, each creating what he believes to be right, each choosing for himself, yet at the same time matching the intentions of others, helping others, with tremendous singleness of purpose. All very paradoxical. And splendid. Dismiss the play as trivial by all means, but give it credit for showing at least some people a vision of possible human behaviour; far more worthwhile than a dozen of your serious dramas or poetic tragedies.

The Victoria Theatre did not become, as had once been envisaged, a good base from which the touring company could set out
on its travels. The main reasons for our finally changing our minds
about this were, firstly, the absence of storage facilities at the new
theatre and in its neighbourhood. Secondly, the financial complications of running a summer season, a touring schedule, and a permanent theatre alarmed various people concerned with our finances:
particularly the Arts Council and several local authorities who contributed to our income. Finally, any repertory company is likely to
find that it grows into the habits and affections of local people; a
visiting company (while the main company were on tour) could not
command the same respect. The financial pressures were decisive
and the directors of the Studio Theatre company reluctantly abandoned Scarborough and the touring company. But the Victoria
Theatre could not resist the temptation of occasional visits to Dartington Hall, or Hemel Hempstead, or LAMDA, or the Questors;
deserting the Victoria no more than two or three times a year.
While the resident company has been away, Peter Cheeseman has
deliberately made the theatre available to amateur groups (the New
Era Players have had full houses for their fine productions of *The
Death of a Salesman* and *The Power and the Glory*), to dance com-
panies (including the Western Theatre Ballet) and, of course, to the
Scarborough company. For though the touring programme vanished,
Scarborough could not be abandoned at once and a new company,
the Scarborough Theatre Trust, took over responsibilities there.

The new company in Scarborough immediately tried to put the
summer seasons on a firmer footing, by negotiating a regular booking
at the Library, by making improvements to the theatre and its
facilities, and by seeking co-operation with the local authority in the
shape of a regular financial grant, of help with publicity, ticket sales
and drawing attention to the existence and place of the theatre. The
corporation were prepared to give a grant, but only on an annual
basis, without any undertaking to repeat it; and they blew hot and
cold on each and every other proposal. The odd thing about Scarborough is that the corporation runs its own theatres and puts on its
own entertainments, and they have never decided if we are a rival
company that should be driven out of town, or a good addition to the
wide range of attractions that a seaside town wants to boast of.
Somewhere between these two extremes is the position from which
no action is taken. And, after another two seasons, it became clear
that a place that was admirable for the first steps, had been outgrown

entirely; and just as there is discomfort in wearing clothes that are too small, and embarrassment in wearing fashions that have just gone out, so the company felt increasingly uncomfortable and unhappy at the Library. We wanted to develop in every way, and, if this was not possible, the sensible alternative seemed to be to abandon Scarborough altogether.

The Stoke theatre has a more promising outlook, but there is no guarantee of permanence. In some ways the element of chanciness encourages hard work, but it also prevents the development of standards and the growth of policy. A now or never situation is unlikely to help artists who are growing in skill and experience. I have learned a good deal from the Victoria Theatre and from the Studio Theatre Ltd, and I am beginning to believe that if theatre in the round is to become, in a significant way, accepted by professional theatre people it will have to be on a grander scale than anything I have done so far.

5
Acting Space and Audience

A MAJOR attraction of theatre in the round is the simplicity with which it can be done. As a form of theatre building, fundamentally nothing at all is required. A plane space provides the central acting area and the room for a surrounding audience. This is the pattern of both the ancient beginnings of theatre and the everyday business of child-play. It is still available for modern, adult and professional performers—if they wish to have theatre at its simplest.

But most of us demand complications, or complications are forced upon us. To start with, it is a bit too ingenuous, in a civilised community, to claim that an empty space is nothing at all. Space costs money. And the sort of space where actors will want to perform to an audience is likely to be very valuable in terms of rent. Further, in England at least, the open air is not often suitable for performances of plays. The climate is usually too cold or wet, and always unreliable. We expect theatres to be indoors. And, having put the actors indoors, artificial lighting becomes available if not always essential.

Perhaps we can stop here for a moment and look at the special requirements of a theatre in the round at this early degree of complication. Our first theatre. It starts with an empty room. Artificial lighting. Accepting that these are ordinary in every way, what must we do to achieve our theatre?

There is one peculiar demand that will probably be made; a modern audience usually expects to sit down. There is no particular reason why they should; it is a recent convention. So for the present, by all means let's bring in chairs for the audience to sit on. They will define the limits of the stage, which is not raised.

The acting area in this minimal theatre should probably be no smaller than 12 ft × 15 ft. On such a stage many plays can be presented; but it is too small for large casts. Fortunately most plays are written in scenes that require only a few characters at a time, and when many people are needed most of them usually form a crowd, dominated by one or two characters. It would be easy to present, say, *Julius Caesar* on a stage this size. Plays where many characters are seen together, all contributing to a kind of symphonic action, might be quite impossible; for example *The Three Sisters*. Of course ballet and opera would be very restricted and virtually unsuited to a stage this size.

Round the acting area, a single row of seats should be arranged, leaving gaps by the doors for use by actors and audience. This suggests a minimum size for the room of eighteen by twenty-one feet, and, allowing for one doorway, you might expect to seat about forty

10. Theatre in the round at its simplest. The drawing is copied (with permission) from a poster designed by Hugo Mazza, advertising a production by Eduardo Malet in Montevideo.

people in your theatre. This reckoning assumes that the seats form a rectangle against the walls of the room. If, in fact, the room is bigger than our minimum, a stage of about the same area surrounded by a circle, an oval or an ellipse of seating would be perfectly feasible. But for simplicity's sake we shall, for the present, consider only rectangular arrangements; most rooms are more or less rectangular.

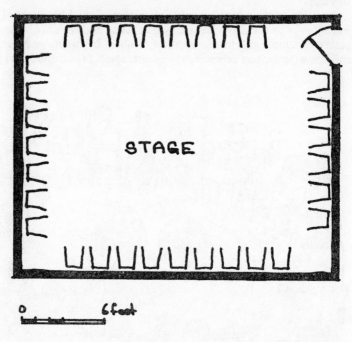

STAGE

0   6 feet

11. Seating plan for converting a room into a theatre.

There is no need to make special arrangements for stage lighting, but since many rooms have a central light fitting it would be helpful to use this scenically—and put up something specially suitable to the play. If the room were to have wall brackets as well, this would be an advantage since lighting only from above tends to make shadows in the actors' eyes, thus giving the audience a poor view of their facial expressions. There is no need, of course, for conventional stage scenery in this or any other theatre in the round. The acting area may be furnished precisely as the room in the play might be furnished. With discrimination, selection or inspiration, it could reflect more or less the locale of the play, even to the extent of a completely empty stage that can be made to seem any place determined by the actors. The completely empty acting area is tremendously attractive and, for many plays, gives the actors absolute freedom to show their skill in building an environment of imagination, a skill exciting to watch in a way that real furnishings seldom are.

A bigger room would offer space for a second row of seats. Roughly speaking, the second row should be 3 ft back from the row in front. So for a complete second row all round the theatre, the room would have to be at least 24 ft × 27 ft. Two rows would provide room for nearly a hundred people.

12. A big room may offer the space for two rows of seats.
But the second row should be higher than the first.

But complications have already arisen. If the acting area is, as we have taken for granted, on the same floor level as the seating, the second row will get a poor view of the actors and the whole purpose of having a theatre at all will be (as, alas, it too often is even in the most elaborate and well established theatres) defeated. The level of the second row must be above the first, preferably by twelve inches or more. Differences in level can be achieved by using different kinds of seating. The front row could be made up of cushions only, or of school gymnasium benches; or, though they would take up more room, easy chairs and settees. The front row could thus be below normal seating height. Alternatively the second row might be raised by sitting on tables, by standing, or by introducing special equipment such as platforms (hardly appropriate in our simplest of theatres).

For a moment let us deal with the common sense of seeing. The object of raising the second row of seats is to enable the people sitting in this row to get a good view of the actors, as has just been said. Put another way, it is a means of providing better sightlines.

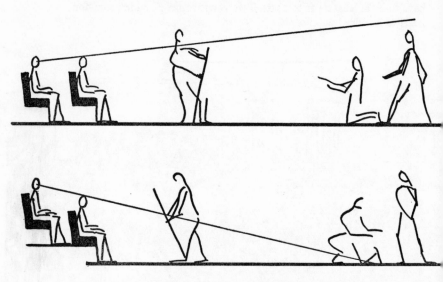

13. Sightline diagram to indicate that two rows on the same level as the acting area give poor vision to the second row, which should therefore be raised.

The term sightline simply means the straight line between the observer's eye and the object he is looking at, and it is important in arranging a theatre because we want everyone to see properly; that is, to have uninterrupted sightlines to the actors. When working out the sightlines on paper we are not usually concerned with the best lines but the worst; we want to find out if the worst is acceptable, and then we can take for granted that the best will be all right. So the two diagrams already drawn only show the sightlines that mark the limits beyond which, from the point of view of a person in the second row, the head of a person in the front row interrupts his view. There is nothing difficult about this, so far. In the diagrams we have taken an acting area about 18 ft across, the second row 3 ft behind the first, an eye-level of 3 ft 8 in. and the distance to the top of the head of a seated person as 4 ft; these last two figures are arbitrary approximations that are generally accepted when working out problems of sightlines. These are vertical measurements, and we are dealing with vertical sightlines. Now an alternative solution is often put forward for the particular problem we are dealing with; it is to stagger the seats, i.e. instead of putting a seat in the second row immediately behind the one in front of it, place it behind the space between adjacent seats. In this way, it is proposed, a person sitting in the second row will see the actors between the heads of the people in front. Obviously there is some sense in this, and under certain

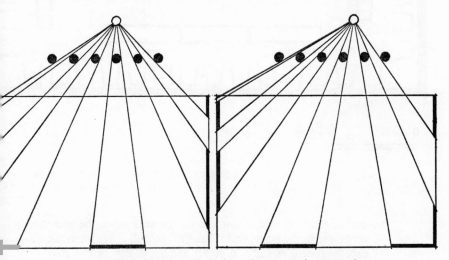

14. Sightline diagram to show that staggering seats does not improve vision when the audience is close to the stage. The black circles represent heads of people in the front row, and sightlines are drawn for only one person in the second row.

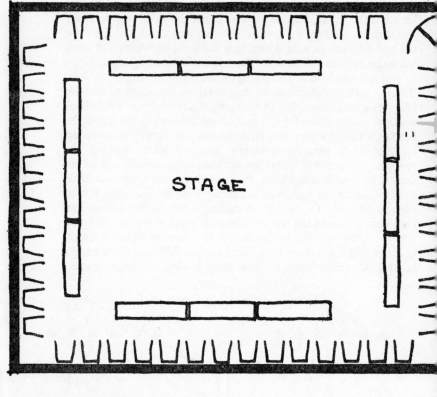

STAGE

0   6 feet

15. Seating plan for Theatre One with two rows of seats.

circumstances it works. But it does not work when the audience is very close to the stage, and it has little overall effect when the audience is spread round the stage: though a few people may have slightly improved sightlines, others have slightly worsened sightlines. The drawings that show this again make use of fairly arbitrary approximations. We can state that, for all practical purposes, there is nothing to be gained by staggering the rows of seats in a small theatre in the round. And even if the seats are staggered the sight-lines of the second row will always be poor unless the row is raised. Let us return to simpler matters.

Here is a theatre capable of seating about a hundred people and presenting all sorts of plays. It only requires actors to bring it to life; and *good* actors might start on a repertoire that need not end till they have in this modest room the most important and enjoyable theatre in the world. This is our first theatre; let us call it, for future reference, Theatre One.

For various reasons, most of us are not attracted by such a possibility and we demand more; a larger theatre, and technical facilities. So let us go on to examine the implications and devise another theatre, which we shall call Theatre Two.

If more than two seating rows are planned it is essential to raise each row above the row in front of it. The step should be at least 1 ft and, presuming that the back-to-back measurement between rows is 3 ft, preferably not less than 1 ft 2 in. It is quite useless to raise only the second row and put a third row on this level. It is useful to raise even the first row above the stage floor, though the measurement here should not be the full step of subsequent rows, and might sensibly equal the intermediate step in the gangways; for example if the vertical difference between levels is 1 ft 2 in., then the gangway should have an intermediate step of 7 in. This would be the height of the front row level above the acting area floor.

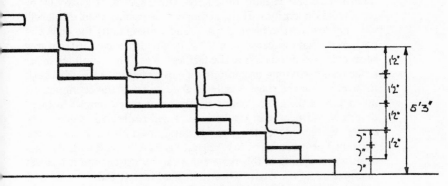

16. Recommended heights for the steps and seating rows in Theatre Two.

In any permanent theatre in the round the seating levels will be part of the main structure, but in a converted hall, or in a small adaptable theatre, they can be made up of portable rostrum units. If rostrum units are sensibly designed they can be used with complete success not only for this purpose, but also for helping to build up other forms of theatre, as well as for scenic constructions. The Victoria Theatre has permanent seating rows. Adaptable theatres can be seen at the Questors and at LAMDA. Sets of rostrums are used to form theatres at such places as Scarborough, Hemel Hempstead, Dartington Hall and St Mary's College, as well as in a growing number of schools and colleges all over the country.

The audience will need stepped access gangways. The width of these may be influenced (as is so much in the design of theatre buildings) by the requirements of the local Fire Officer who has absolute authority over matters relating to public safety. Four feet six inches may be taken as a reasonable measurement. But though these gangways are necessary, actors will need to approach the acting area without any change in level. Indeed, in every kind of theatre, it is desirable that even the dressing rooms should be on the same level as the stage. For actors' access, steps and slopes are nuisances, and if they cannot be avoided they should be kept as far away as possible from the acting area itself. However, since a theatre in the round must have stepped gangways, these should be planned to provide the actor with additional approaches to the stage.

A theatre in the round of the larger size we are now considering will, of course, have an acting area bigger than that of Theatre One. The precise size is hard to specify. But 18 ft × 21 ft would be reasonable dimensions. If the acting area is smaller than this it will not only restrict the playing space (and consequently the choice of play, as we have already noted), but it will also make the front row seem cramped in relation to the farthest rows. This cramping effect is the result of wrong proportions; it can be felt in the Scarborough theatre, where the stage is only 12 ft × 16 ft. If the acting area is much bigger than our present suggestion it may often seem to be deserted, and people in the back rows will really feel remote from actors on the side of the stage farthest from them. Even at the Victoria Theatre, where the acting area is 24 ft × 22 ft with six rows of seats, something of this remoteness can be sensed, and it features in criticisms of the Arena Theatre in Washington DC.

Theatre Two will need, say, three or four entrances for the actors at stage level. Besides the additional entrances provided by the

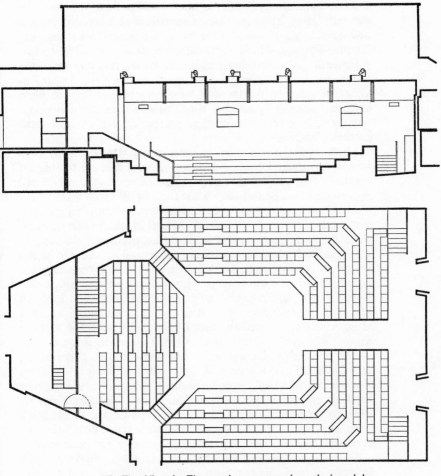

17. The Victoria Theatre is a conversion, designed by Stephen Joseph, from an old cinema.

audience gangways, it is useful to have entrances from below. All or part of the stage floor may be trapped so that such an entrance can be made wherever is most suitable for the particular production. Entrances from above, though less often required, have always been useful in the theatre, and the requirement should not be ignored when designing the ceiling and roof space of a theatre in the round.

The actual capacity of this playhouse could be decided to suit local demands. Here, let us examine an example to seat between 350 and 400 people. There would have to be six seating rows, and our Theatre Two would have plan measurements of about 54 ft × 57 ft. An overall floor area bigger than this would probably make the theatre too large for the presentation of modern plays. An ancient Greek or medieval theatre may have been bigger, but our plays could not sensibly be acted in them; though it would be perfectly reasonable (certainly not ideal) to present their plays in a small modern playhouse.

I base my choice of size on the experience of watching many plays in many theatres. I have often found theatres that are too big for plays, allowing people at the back to have an unsatisfactorily diluted impression of the performance while those in the first few rows have a falsely enlarged version of the same show. In many big theatres, seats in the first five rows are very difficult to sell. And no matter if there are many good seats, it is clearly impossible for the actor to give a performance that is satisfactory from every part of too large a theatre. It is wrong to be too dogmatic about this. My experience is essentially personal and some people are clearly satisfied with a view from the gods, while others gladly occupy the front rows. I am not anxious to generalise for all theatres and all audiences. If pressed I must retreat to the defence that I am striving to define a single theatre, and in this theatre it is especially required that the actor should be able to give a more or less homogeneous performance, seen and heard by every member of the audience. I have seldom been in a theatre that actually seemed too small (though often the audience has been embarrassingly small in a big theatre—but that's another question). And the Arena Theatre at Tufts College in Medford, Massachusetts, seating 200 people, seemed to me to be a little gem. If one wants to seat more than this it is mainly for economic reasons.

In designing Theatre Two, I have, of course, been thinking mostly in terms of professional theatre. Actors and writers must be paid. In England the theatre still depends very much on its ticket sales and what little money the treasury gives to the Arts Council goes more to opera and ballet than to drama; and the drama's claims are louder from the National Theatre and other big companies than from small groups. Small theatres can expect little help. I am not sure that I want to complain about this. Perhaps it is right that an independent theatre, striving to achieve high artistic ideals, should have to prove itself by more or less balancing its own accounts, while well-known theatres should be allowed a comparative degree of luxury and waste. To survive in spite of great obstacles is the most convincing way of proving the validity of the ideals, perhaps. But if some theatres are subsidised and some not, there will be unfair competition in markets where they all go—to find actors, for instance. These aspects of theatre business are too specialised to warrant full treatment here. But they do essentially tend to push our seating capacity higher than we might otherwise wish.

If we choose a capacity that can be contained in five or six rows, I believe the central stage now gives the actor a reasonable chance of making a fully satisfying communication with everyone in the audience. More than half a dozen rows begin to impose a strain on this communication. In a conventional theatre, with a proscenium arch, half a dozen rows would not accommodate many people; and it is one of the main strengths of theatre in the round that in fairly limited distance from the stage a comparatively large audience can be contained, thus making not only a practical proposition of a mere five rows but also a valid testing ground for the actor who can aim his performance equally to several hundred people and not just to a clique. Numbers do not mean everything, but at least they can be more easily assimilated than aesthetic theories. And, for what they are worth, here are comparative figures showing how many people can be accommodated in the first five rows of several existing theatres; the three columns of figures show, first the total seating capacity of the theatre in question, second the number of seats in the first five rows, and finally the relationship between them expressed as a percentage so that you can compare at once the proportion of seats contained in the first five rows in theatres of different sizes:

Sadlers Wells	1,523	126	8·3
Chichester	1,360	262	19·3
Her Majesty's	1,319	108	8·2
Saville	1,200	113	9·4
Aldwych	1,024	94	9·2
Haymarket	901	71	8·0
Ashcroft	725	63	8·4
Royal Court	405	79	19·5
Victoria, Stoke	345	311	90·1
Scarborough	248	248	100·0
Hampstead	160	80	50·0

The theatres are listed in order of size, and by comparing the total capacities with the final percentages you can discern a tendency, to be expected, for the smaller theatres to have a larger percentage of seats in the first five rows; and a theatre with only five rows will obviously have 100%—as Scarborough does. On the other hand the larger theatres do not necessarily have the larger numbers of seats in the front. Stoke comes out best from this second column test, and it is one of the smaller theatres. Then comes Chichester, a big theatre, and then Scarborough; the others are in a different bracket altogether. This shows, again as one would expect, that the thrust stage and theatre in the round manage to provide larger seating capacities in the front rows than conventional theatres, with theatre in the round having the advantage, total capacities permitting. Finally, the last entries in the table clearly show that when small theatres are considered, theatre in the round has a substantial lead even over the open-end stage when it comes to getting its audience within a limited distance of the stage—and thus achieving the homogeneous performance we have been aiming at. There is much information to be got from these figures and I suspect a statistician could prove all sorts of things from them—including much to my dis-comfort—but surely the simple message is clear?

In none of our three theatres so far have we considered the possibility of a raised stage which, after all, is one of the common characteristics of most theatres. Perhaps it is worth emphasising that for all ordinary purposes a theatre in the round should not have a raised stage because of the resulting difficulties in seeing the actors and, relatedly, in lighting them; difficulties that will become apparent when we discuss setting and lighting. However, there are certain circumstances when a raised stage may be appropriate for a theatre in the round. For example if an informal theatre is arranged for a few performances only, and particularly if it is out of doors, the elaborate business of getting seating rows may be avoided by raising the stage instead. For a daylight performance and for a play where no furniture or other objects need be set on the stage, the sightlines will not be subjected to too much strain. However, the actors will seem to mask each other all the time, and a well-raised stage, which in any theatre always gives a very false view of the actors to people in the first few rows, hardly recommends itself in a theatre where most of the audience will be contained in only a few rows. In addi-tion, theatre in the round will present an unavoidably false per-spective view, forcing us, as it were, to watch Juliet through the legs of Romeo. We may be prepared to put up with such shortcomings if there are good reasons for not doing things better.

But another set of circumstances may demand the best we can devise even with a raised stage; suppose that we have to design an opera house. This would become Theatre Three. There are many examples in the United States, ranging from the beautiful and substantial geodesic dome that houses the Casa Mañana in Fort Worth, Texas, to tent theatres that offer summer season shows. Musicals are usually presented, occasionally opera and ballet and even (though not always appropriately) straight plays.

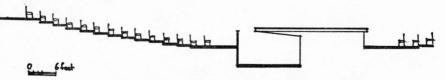

18. Part section (omitting further seating rows to the right) through a theatre in the round with a raised stage and orchestra pit. The plan would be circular, accommodating about 2,000 people.

For such entertainments a large audience may be catered for; say two thousand in fourteen rows. Now the raising of fourteen rows, each a foot or more higher than the one in front, would make for an uncomfortably high viewpoint towards the back of the theatre, and, perhaps, an awkwardly high ceiling. A compromise provides the sensible answer. A slightly stepped auditorium 4 in. or 6 in. each row (steeper at the back than at the front), or a sloping floor at a gradient of not more than 1 in 10 (public safety rules out a steeper slope)—and a raised stage, say 3 ft 6 in. above datum level, which we can conveniently take as the level of the floor on which the front row is placed. The strained upward view of a close front row can best be alleviated by having a "no-man's-land" between stage and auditorium, and this will also lessen our stage lighting difficulties. In part of "no-man's-land" between stage and auditorium, at about 4 ft below datum level, carrying on under the stage, an orchestra pit is easily accommodated. Stage furniture will still be a nuisance, but this is primarily a musical theatre and, when the chorus is kicking, not much furniture is required, and masking presents no problems. The attraction of a circle of dancing girls is obvious enough, and most opera house theatres in the round are circular in plan.

6
Lighting and Sound

Lighting

STAGE lighting for theatre in the round is a difficult subject to write on succinctly since there has been little opportunity for people to gain the experience from which a reasonable body of facts might be collected. But in theory there is a very wide range of possibilities, and there is plenty of scope for people to disagree. However, by limiting these notes to cover the particular experiences gained from one series of lighting installations, and only slightly considering other arrangements, a reasonable degree of clarity may be achieved. We can further clarify our suggestions by applying them to the theatres described in the last chapter. Of course the recommendations will often be arbitrary and dogmatic, but where they are so the alternatives should appear the more readily.

Perhaps it ought to be mentioned first that in this country it is usually required that a public theatre should have a secondary or emergency lighting system and that the lights from this system, as well as the exit lights, should be on all the time an audience is in the theatre. This requirement is likely to be awkward in the comparatively small volume of a theatre in the round, making it impossible to achieve a blackout on the acting area, which will remain lit even when the stage lighting is out. If the Chief Fire Officer agrees, a reasonable alternative is to install a secondary lighting system that comes on automatically when there is a mains failure and may be switched on at other times if required; such systems are readily available. Again, the Fire Chief may agree to specially restricted lighting focused on to gangways, which, together with exit lights will provide sufficient spill into the rest of the auditorium for reasonable safety in emergencies. This is a matter of commonsense and co-operation between the people concerned.

The notes that follow are based on a specific system. Much of it derives from experience of lighting proscenium stages, though neither these nor other forms of open stage are considered here. The basic idea of our systematic approach comes from *A Method of Lighting the Stage* by Stanley McCandless (but theatre in the round is not touched on in this excellent little book).* As far as possible the separate factors of the system will be given in a logical order, but their value may only become manifest when the whole series of notes is considered together.

Firstly, the lighting for the theatre in the round will normally come from spotlights. Floodlights and battens have virtually no application and will not be further mentioned. The most suitable lantern is a soft edge spotlight with a fresnel lens and a beam that can be adjusted within the approximate limits of 15° and 45° and using a 500-watt lamp; for example, the Strand pattern 123 baby fresnel spot is ideal. In theatres of the smallest sort a 250-watt lamp may be used in this lantern; and for theatres of the largest size the fresnel spot Strand pattern 243 with a 1,000 watt lamp may be preferred.

Profile spots and other lanterns and lamps may also be useful, and attention will be drawn to them when they might be preferred. But the general scheme can be most simply described by restricting reference to one sort of lantern. Note that the Strand pattern 264 uses a 1,000-watt lamp and has adjustable hard/soft edges, very useful for theatre in the round work, though it is likely to remain more expensive than the ordinary soft edge lantern.

Next, let us see where the spotlights should be placed. When working out the ideal positions for spotlights ensure that in elevation the angle between the horizontal and the beam of light need be no more than about 45°. If it is much more than 50° awkward shadows begin to be formed, particularly round the actors' eyes. Note that this applies in any form of theatre, but don't forget that it may be an effect positively required on special occasions. The angle can be less than 45°, but if it is much less than 25° difficulty may be experienced in keeping direct light out of the eyes of the audience.

* Stanley McCandless, *A Method of Lighting the Stage* (Theatre Arts Books).

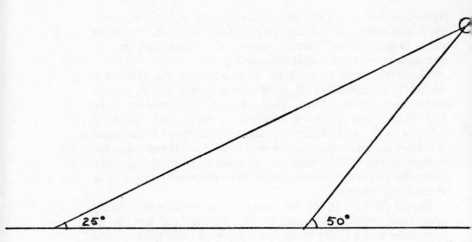

19. The open circle represents a spotlight, and the lines from it show the beam of light. It is recommended that the beam should strike the horizontal at no more than 50°, and no less than 25°, as indicated.

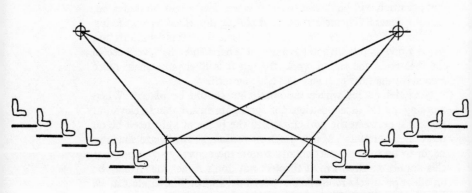

20. If the spotlights can be carefully sited round the acting area there need be no steep angles of lighting nor spill into the audience's eyes, and only a few lanterns need be used. The next drawing suggests some lay-outs in plan.

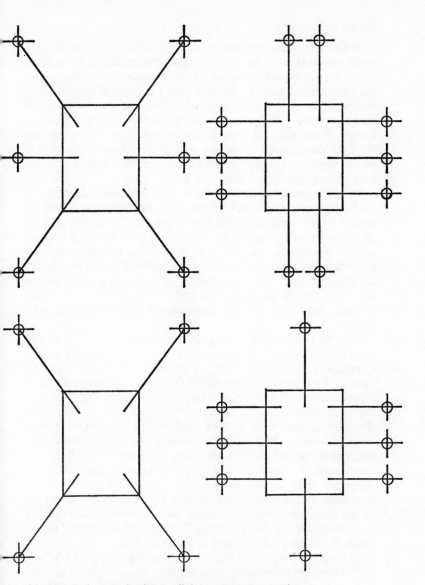

21. Plans of very simple spotlight arrangements using from four to ten lanterns. Notice that the spotlights are not directly over the acting area but outside it. (*Drawn by John Jones.*)

In the sort of theatres we are dealing with, the throw of these spotlights (that is to say the distance between the lamp and the object lit) will probably be about 20 ft. Note that this distance and the beam angle required will mean that a substantial proportion of the spotlights are positioned not so much over the acting area as over the seating rows—and probably towards the outer walls of the auditorium. When calculating positions for spotlights, remember that the light should cover the actors, and in elevational drawings it is worth taking a line about 5 ft above the acting area level and ensuring that beam angles spread along this line.

With this data let us now get down to the business of lighting our smallest theatre in the round, Theatre One. As long as the room is big enough to give us a reasonable throw, only four spotlights need be used, one in each corner of the room, shining down at an angle as near to the ideal as we can get it. This is minimal stage lighting equipment, but a real technical advance on the domestic lighting we allowed earlier on. More ambitious lighting schemes might involve six, eight or ten spotlights arranged round the room as shown. In each case 250-watt lamps in pattern 123 spotlights should be used.

Now let us see what is required for Theatre Two, a medium-sized theatre, with an acting area of 18 ft × 21 ft. It needs a more complicated lay-out, and here our system begins to come into its own. Roughly speaking this consists of dividing the acting area into separate units each of which will be lit independently but employing the same relative lantern lay-out. Beam angles in elevation have already been dealt with. In plan a satisfactory distribution of spotlights is achieved by having 120° separation. Alternative arrangements, such as 90° or 60° separation, are perfectly possible, with their particular advantages and snags, but 120° is recommended for simplicity, efficiency and economy and will be the only plan dealt with here. Each area unit, then, is lit by three spotlights and a stage of our size is probably best divided into six areas, thus requiring eighteen spotlights. These eighteen lights should be arranged to give minimal spill into the audience, as shown in 22.

This series of unit areas will enable the whole stage to be fully lit with a fairly even spread of light. Separate areas can be lit in isolation, or varying degrees of brightness given to different areas by using dimmer control. All the spotlights used for lighting the unit areas will normally be set for optimum effect and left from one production to the next without any adjustment.

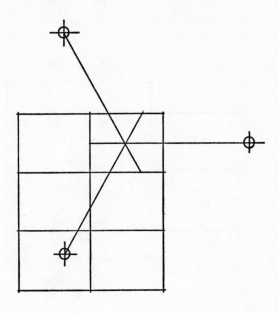

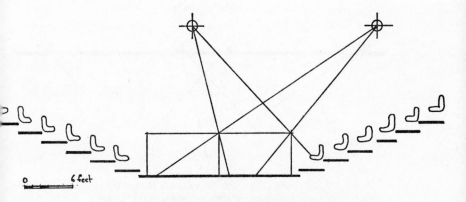

0 ———— 6 feet

22. The upper diagram is a plan showing the stage divided into six areas, one of which has the three spotlights, separated by 120°, recommended for each area. The lower diagram shows the beam angles in section, in relation to the area (or, more importantly, a line five feet above stage level) and to the seating.

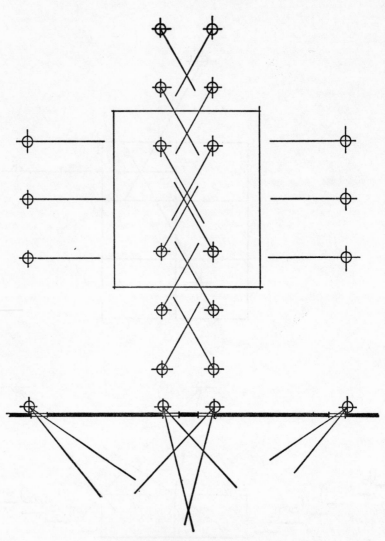

23. The upper diagram is a plan of the eighteen spotlights used for lighting the area units. They are shown in relation to the stage (and note that only four spotlights are actually over the stage), and would normally be placed in the ceiling void; the section shows how the spotlights shine through gaps in the ceiling. The gaps are best made in the form of long troughs, four of which would be required, running vertically on our plan.

Extra lighting may be useful to cover entrances and to increase the definition of the acting area, and further lighting troughs may be necessary for these purposes. Extra lighting will be required for such purposes as indicating sunlight (and possibly a specially powerful lantern), artificial light from on-stage lamps, specially confined areas, and for colour effects. It is not possible to anticipate all the needs of many different plays, but a sensible calculation can be based on the provision of a dozen extra spotlights for these purposes; use profile spotlights in each case; and, since these extra lights may be wanted in various places, allow for a dozen spare circuits as well.

A good profile spotlight is the Strand pattern 23 which bears a family resemblance to the 123 used so far. This spotlight gives its most efficient light with a beam of about 22°, with a hard edge, i.e. there is a sharp contrast between the exact area lit and the immediately surrounding area. The beam can be narrowed, or shaped by placing special metal slides with various shaped cut-outs (these are diaphragms) into a gate between the lens and the lamp. A diffuser glass can easily be positioned in front of the lens to provide a soft edge when required.

Our theatre now has thirty spotlights, and forty-two available positions. Since theatre in the round can handle plays in repertoire with comparative ease (not having the scenic storage problem of a proscenium theatre), this may be part of its policy—as it is at the Victoria Theatre. Allow about six extra spotlights for each play in repertoire, up to a maximum of thirty. The total number of spotlights has now reached sixty. It is not anticipated that all spotlights will be used at any one time, but the control to be described will provide for easy selection.

In Theatre Two each spotlight position should be provided with an adjacent socket outlet. Thus for our sixty spotlights, we have seventy-two outlets and circuits. Spotlights are normally equipped with 2 ft 6 in. tails of heat-resistant cable to which plugs must be fitted. Use three-pin 5-amp plugs and sockets throughout the system. Each socket outlet should be on cable trunking so that there is no loose cable. The trunking will lead directly into the control room where a connecting panel will provide separate flexible leads for each circuit and carry them to a plug board associated with a patch panel.

The plug board should reproduce the pattern of sockets outlets; each circuit should be appropriately wired into the board, ending in a standard plug.

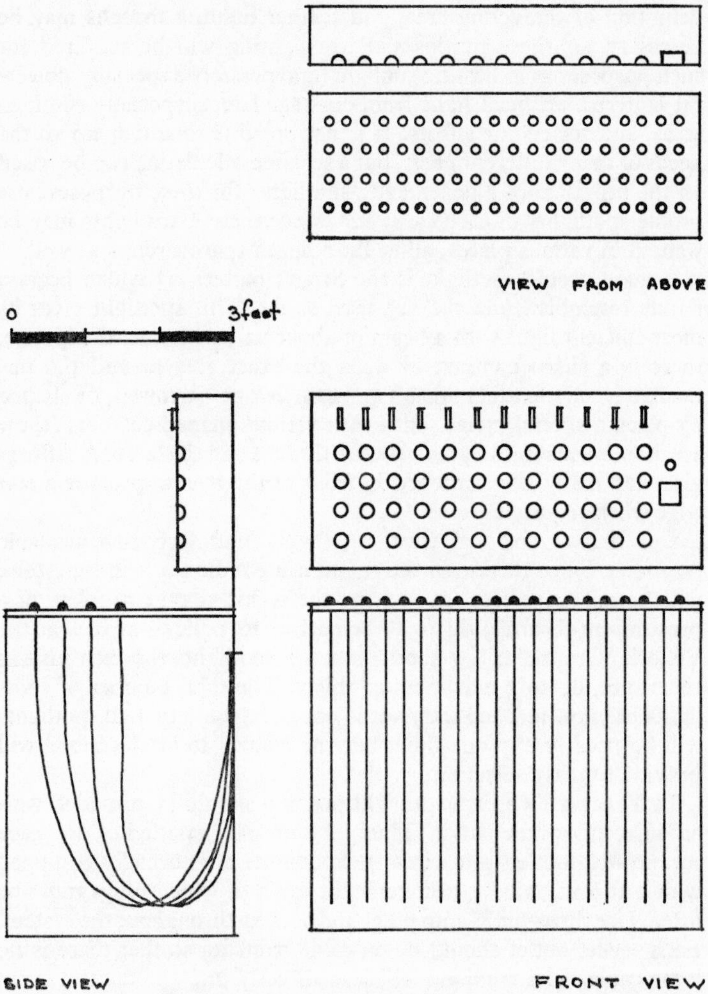

VIEW FROM ABOVE

0   3 feet

SIDE VIEW

FRONT VIEW

24. Plug board and associated patch panel showing how 80 spotlight circuits may be associated with a control board of twelve dimmers. Each dimmer controls up to 4 circuits, allowing a maximum of 48 circuits under dimmer control at any time.

Since each area unit consists of three spotlights, these should be controlled by a single dimmer. On the patch panel a vertical row of sockets should be wired to each dimmer. In practice four rather than three sockets can be provided for each row; resistance dimmers are available to cope with a variable load of 1,000/2,000 watts, and special lights may often be used in relation to particular area units. A total of twelve dimmers will be satisfactory for the sort of installation we have been describing. It allows up to forty-eight of the sixty available spotlights to be used at any one time. Further, the patch panel can be employed for rearrangements of the lights under control not only for each play but also, if required, during a play from cue to cue. Thus all sixty spotlights might be used during a single performance. This is modest stuff, appropriate to Theatre Two. More ambitious schemes will give extra ease and flexibility of control, and these advantages will be apparent to anyone who knows about stage lighting. The control described here will suit the beginner who is still learning to understand the problems of control—and will be perfectly efficient in action.

The arrangement at the Victoria Theatre consists of seventy-two circuits, forty-four spotlights and eight dimmers. All spotlights are powered at 500 watts. The resistance dimmers are rated at 1,500 watts plus or minus one-third, and each is linked to four socket outlets. A total of thirty-two outlets can therefore be controlled at any one time. At the Pembroke Theatre, in Croydon, between thirty-six and forty spotlights were normally used; in Scarborough the control consisted of four dimmers, each handling four circuits from a patch panel with twenty-two outlets, and there were usually about sixteen spotlights available.

The control room will probably contain both lighting and sound effects control apparatus; it should overlook the acting area, giving operators an unobstructed view of the entire stage. A long window of reasonable height, to give a good view to a standing person in the control room, should be provided. A high degree of sound insulation is necessary between control room and auditorium, but at least part of the window should open to allow direct speech between operators and producer during rehearsals.

The actual business of lighting a play will depend entirely on the approach preferred by each producer. When working in a repertory theatre I prefer to start from the systematic illumination of the entire acting area so that I know I always have good basic illumination available to serve many different productions. For this purpose

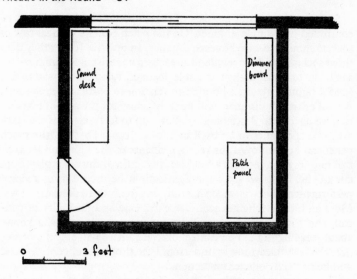

Sound desk

Dimmer board

Patch panel

0   3 feet

25. Suggested lay-out for a control room that houses
lighting and sound equipment.

the acting area is divided into a number of sections, as already indicated. The three spots for each section are linked at the patch panel
to a single dimmer and with all dimmers full on, the whole acting
area is well lit and the light fairly evenly spread. Changes in emphasis
can be obtained by lowering the light intensity in one or more areas,
and, of course, any area can be left unlit. Over this basic lighting,
with its variable application I now begin to plot the extra lights
needed. Not much work is required as a rule to arrive at as complex a
schedule as any play may demand. I am a lazy person and like to get
technical matters done as swiftly and as efficiently as possible. I don't
share the common enthusiasm among technicians for staying up all
night to do the lighting; indeed, I have come to recognise that the
staying up all night attitude usually gives poor results, and is no
more than a case of persistence trying to stand in for knowledge and
efficiency. In my opinion the capabilities of the spotlight lay-out
should be studied before lighting a play, and without even a play in
mind; once you really know what each of your spotlights can do the
lighting plot can easily be worked out on paper and quickly trans-
ferred from paper to the instruments themselves.

The use of colour filters is a personal affair. They do not seem to me to be so much required for theatre in the round as for the picture-frame stage. For the latter, secondary colour filters may help to give three-dimensional clarity, but for theatre in the round no such aid is needed. In certain plays, particularly expressionistic or abstract works, strong colours may be of use, but they should be selected carefully as a fundamental contribution to the total visual impact of the production. Coloured light modifies the colour of costumes and the colour of flesh, and its effects are powerful enough to require very careful handling. A novice should remember that any colour filter reduces the amount of effective light, and that moonlight is not blue, firelight is not red, and above all that an audience expects to see actors acting.

It is not easy, in a small theatre, to keep one area brilliantly lit and another completely dark, as the dust particles in the atmosphere tend to spread even the most rigid beams of light, and whatever the beam strikes, even if only the floor, a certain amount of reflection is sure to occur. The difficulty is accentuated in theatre in the round where spotlights shine from widely separated angles; and the requirement of an isolated pool of light is probably best met by using only one or two specially focused spotlights for the necessary effect; it is not an effect often wanted. Extra spotlights can be used to bring added intensity to any section or object in the acting area; entrances, windows, or sources of artificial light in the setting may require punching up in this way.

If you are converting a hall into a theatre in the round, it may not be possible to find ideal positions for the spotlights. At the Library Theatre in Scarborough a compromise had to be reached, since the cornice dictated where we must put the surrounding ring of lights, and not much variation could be played on the possible positions of a temporary overhead grid suspended from the ceiling laylights. But where possible, particularly if a theatre in the round is being planned on an architect's drawing board, the lanterns should be placed in the roof void (or lighting loft), the whole of which may be floored over— or walkways constructed adjacent to the rows of spotlights. Handrails should be provided for safety. Spotlights can be suspended from 2 in. scaffolding tubes or mounted on base plates; there are a number of possible arrangements that will provide both the necessary facilities for access to the lanterns and give the desired beam angles. Details will depend on the precise design of the ceiling structure, and it is only important to ensure that the spotlights can in fact be easily handled, and that they can be directed properly to give the beam angles we have described.

A satisfactory arrangement for a theatre with a circular plan, such as Theatre Three, will rely on two circular troughs in the lighting loft using roughly the same scheme for area units already indicated. In this particular case not one of the lanterns is placed directly over the acting area. It is worth repeating this because it is commonly assumed that theatre in the round lighting comes solely from directly over the acting area, a scheme that could provide nothing but inadequate or very peculiar illumination for the actors.

Nowadays it is usually accepted that lighting should be used to help focus the audience's attention on the stage; and the auditorium lighting is dimmed before the stage lights come up, to assist this effect. A common criticism of theatre in the round is that you can see the audience opposite you. It is true, you can. Yet it is amusing that when you come to select photographs of theatre in the round, the choice is hard to make because most action pictures show only the actors; you cannot see the audience and therefore get no clear indication that there is a central stage. Flashlight photographs show both actors and audience, but to interrupt a performance with flashes is not fair to anyone and the results look artificial. Overexposure may show the audience, but the actors will be meaningless blurs of black and white. Specially posed photographs can be taken with the lighting balanced to show the seating (if not an actual audience) as well as the actors, but then the actors, encouraged by their natural instincts as well as by the photographer, tend to project in a linear direction towards the camera, thus losing the organic projection that is fundamental to theatre in the round.

Good photographs, then, are hard to get. Of course the human eye is simultaneously sensitive to light over a wider range than most cameras, and we can easily choose what we want to look at. Thus, if you *want* to look at the audience opposite, you may do so: and, if this proves your point against theatre in the round, I suppose you have had your money's worth of entertainment. Again, when the play or the acting becomes dull, perhaps it is no bad alternative to have a number of human faces to take up your interest. In my estimation, the majority of people who go to theatre in the round accept the sea of faces, just as easily as they accept the sea of heads in conventional theatres and cinemas, and concentrate on the acting as soon as it begins. Lighting helps. Even so, there may be times

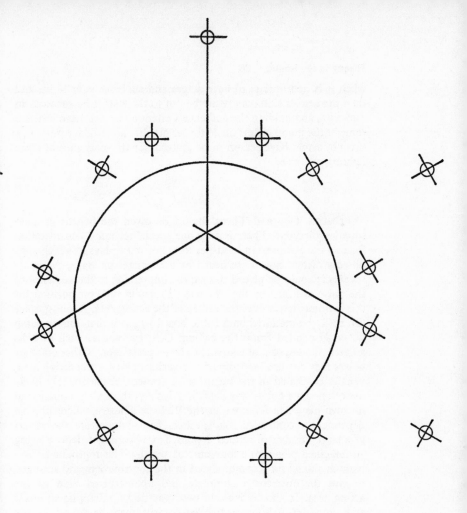

26. Spotlight lay-out plans for Theatre Three. The principle
is the same as for rectangular acting areas, except that the
circle is divided into six segments, and each of these area
units is lit by three spotlights. Using the same measurements as before (see drawing on page 79), we find that
the lanterns are disposed in two circles and they are shown
here in relation to the stage; they would be placed in the
ceiling void, and there would be two circular lighting
troughs. There are no spotlights immediately over the acting
area, though a more complex lay-out might make good use
of them. (*Drawn by John Jones.*)

D

when it is appropriate to have actors and audience equally lit, and then the actor's skill may really be put to the test; if he succeeds in capturing and holding the audience's attention he will have justified some of the grand claims made for his art. For all ordinary purposes, though, actors have reason to be grateful for the assistance of stage lighting well used.

Sound

Theatres Two and Three should be given the benefit of good sound equipment. There is only one special technical consideration for us—the positions of loudspeakers. For most plays in which supposedly distant noises are heard by a character on stage, the loudspeakers should be placed to give the impression to the audience of the noise as heard by the character. Probably the best position for this is immediately over the centre of the acting area. A loudspeaker can easily be mounted on a baffle board which is then incorporated in, or suspended from, the ceiling. On-stage noises, such as bells and telephones, can, of course, be rigged practicably. Other on-stage noises may require loudspeakers in various parts of the acting area, usually concealed in the furniture or scenery. A particularly lively use of on-stage noises was made in Alan Ayckbourn's production of his own play, *Mr Whatnot*, at the Victoria Theatre, where five independently controlled loudspeakers helped to create the effects of a large number of mimed actions, from opening a door, playing an imagined piano, to a foursome at tennis. The reproducing apparatus should be accommodated in the control room and arranged to give the operator a complete and unobstructed view of the acting area. It should include two tape-decks, microphone, mixer and amplifier. Although this equipment may be found in any theatre, the control is likely to be expensive and complicated, so once again, for the sake of simplicity, a few further remarks may be helpful.

The reason for having two decks is so that sound effects can be mixed from two different tapes, both running at the same time or overlapping smoothly. The decks should be sturdy and easy to use. Piano key controls are not satisfactory. The controls should be mechanically silent. A good pause switch (and preferably one that can be locked), or an instant stop/start control, is essential. The heads should be two-track mono, and two or three speeds should be available. It should be easy to lace the tape, and the point of impact with the playing head should be easily seen so as to facilitate accurate cueing. I know of no reasonably priced tape-deck that comes up to these specifications. Most machines are noisy in operation, the playback head is difficult to see, the pause switch is clumsy, or the controls are fragile. Not even the famous Warerite deck of the Ferrograph is good enough, but either this or the Brennell Mark 5 (which has a poor pause switch), will probably be best.

If the amplifier is separate from the mixer it should have set controls, and it can be positioned away from the control top. All gain controls should be on the mixer. Most control knobs are designed for domestic use; for theatre purposes a gain control should be big enough to handle firmly yet finely, the knob itself should be marked with numbered settings to align with a pointer on the instrument panel; or the control should be a lever. The best instruments for the job, as far as I know, are the Vortexion 10/15-watt mixer-amplifier and the Phillips series 1045. These handle signals from four sources. Such mixer-amplifiers can be custom-made to suit various specified inputs.

Provision should be made for enclosing the tape-decks in cases that have flush decks, and lids with transparent tops of Perspex; the mixer-amplifier is probably best mounted on a rack over the desk that carries the tape-decks. Panels should also be provided, one switch and socket distributor for mains supply to each instrument, and the other an output control to loudspeakers, with a safety device to bring in load when all speakers are off.

These various requirements can usually be met by ordinary domestic apparatus and there is no need to buy elaborate and costly instruments, though these may be helpful if there is both money to spare and a skilled person to handle the equipment.

The apparatus so far described serves the purpose of playing sound effects, incidental music and so on. The business of preparing the effects should be done quite separately and, if possible, in a studio (even if this is only an ordinary room). The studio should have a good tape recorder, record player, microphone and a mixer. The tape-decks from the control room should be brought into the studio when it is necessary to record from a tape, though an extra deck will be helpful.

A more complicated lay-out will make use of two amplifiers, and will provide extra facilities such as the ability to have two sound effects simultaneously coming from different speakers; and a paging system from the control room to dressing rooms, foyer or backstage;

or playback from on-stage to the dressing rooms. A schematic diagram shows how this can easily be done. It is sensible to have each of the mixer-amplifiers the same so that control can easily be switched from one to the other.

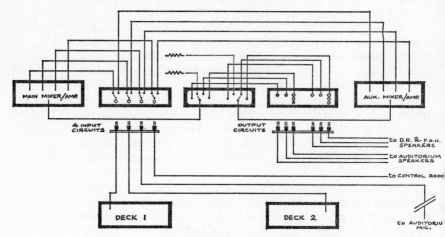

27. Schematic drawing to show sound reproducing equipment for Theatre Two. Four input signals are allowed for: two from tape decks, one from control room microphone and one from auditorium microphone (probably suspended centrally over the acting area). The circuits from these are fed via a plug board (like the common telephone control board) to a control panel that can switch each signal either to the main or auxiliary amplifier. Here, mixer/amplifiers are used; these provide volume and tone controls. The amplified sound now goes to a second control panel that provides for the selection of output circuits, and a third control panel in conjunction with a plug board allows choice of loudspeakers. (*Drawn by John Jones.*)

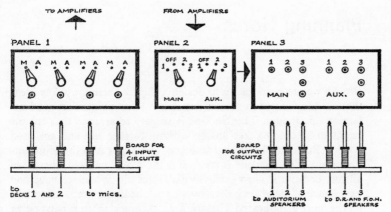

28. Detail to show switching facilities provided by the control panels incorporated in the scheme of the previous drawing. These panels will have to be specially made, and they might well be arranged as a single unit in three sections. The first panel has four sockets, to take the jack-plugs from the signal sources, and four two-position dipole switches to send each signal to either main or auxiliary amplifier. Panel two has two four-position dipole switches; one switch handles the sound from the main and the other from the auxiliary amplifier. Three of the four positions lead to panel three, while the remainder is an *off* position with resistor loading. Panel three consists of socket outlets into which loudspeaker jack-plugs can be inserted. The sockets are in two similar groups, one fed from the main and the other from the auxiliary amplifier. Sockets 1 and 2 are connected with positions 1 and 2 of the corresponding switch on panel 2; position 3 leads to three linked outlets. There can thus be a choice of three separate speakers, or up to three speakers in circuit together. Sockets 1 and 2, and one socket of the linked three, should be resistor loaded when the plug is withdrawn. (*Drawn by John Jones.*)

7
Planning Notes

BEFORE we are quite ready to design a theatre there are a few ideas that need looking at in greater detail, and a few points that need enlarging on; though Theatre One is so easy to arrange that anyone ought to be able to take charge without further ado and get good results. But don't be misled into supposing that it is therefore unimportant. The opposite is true—it is the most important theatre of all just because it is so easily available for all. When we have had experience of many such theatres we shall be better prepared to take on the more complicated Theatre Two; technical matters need never be a barrier between us and activity, especially if that activity is acting. But when we've done a good deal of acting in Theatre One it is more than likely that we shall want to master the technical matters that will help us to achieve Theatre Two.

Theatre Two can be built either with permanent raised levels for the seating rows or with portable rostrum units. It is the latter that we shall now examine in greater detail. For with the aid of these rostrums almost any hall of about the right size can become our theatre. It is only a little more complicated than Theatre One, but it provides us with stage and auditorium good enough for the best of actors and audiences.

There are a number of different ways of making rostrums, but the best for our purposes is the standard parallel. It is quite tricky to make, but since it is very commonly used to build up stage levels, most big firms who supply scenery and stage fittings can provide them without detail drawings; they will simply want to know the overall measurements.

In designing rostrums for our purpose, modules should be decided on and all rostrums then built so that they are as far as possible interchangeable. This will make the business of putting them up and

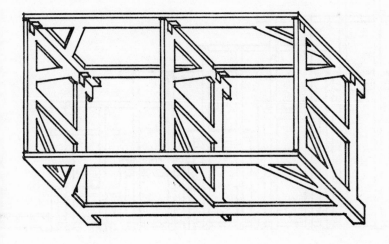

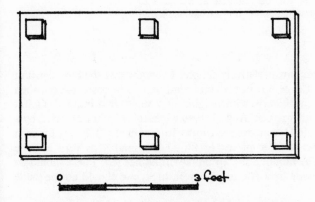

0   3 feet

29. Standard parallel. The blocks on the underside of the top locate in the corners of the framework, helping to keep it firm.

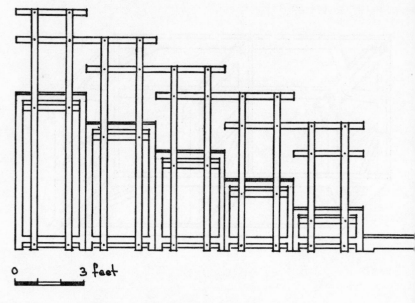

30. Handrails will be required at the side of a tier of
    rostrums unless it butts against a wall.

taking them down relatively simple. I suggest that the modular unit
should be 3 ft × 6 ft in plan and 7 in. high. The rostrums can then
be built conveniently with heights of 7 in., 1 ft 9 in., 2 ft 11 in.,
4 ft 1 in. and 5 ft 3 in. Any of these when folded can be carried by a
normal adult. One or two rostrums with a plan of 3 ft × 3 ft for each
height, and smaller pieces to fill in the final gaps may also be
necessary. A number of step units will be needed. These should be
4 ft 6 in. wide by 1 ft 6 in. and 7 in. high, and should not be made
to fold.

Handrails will be required where the sides of the rostrums are
exposed, and if the backs of the highest level of rostrums do not butt
on to the walls backrails will also be necessary. The best way of
making these is of 3-in. × 1-in. timber. Horizontal pieces should be
cut in 6-ft lengths (with a few 3-ft lengths); vertical pieces should be
4 ft 3 in., 5 ft 5 in., 6 ft 7 in. and 7 ft 9 in. Clamping pieces about

2 ft 10 in. long should be cut to fit inside the rostrum units. These pieces are drilled at standard intervals to take $\frac{1}{2}$-in. coach bolts and assembled as shown. To help with rigidity pieces of hardboard can be clamped between the verticals and horizontal at the bottom of each run of handrails.

These handrails are not a standard scenic item and they will have to be home made or ordered in detail. I think I can claim, for what it is worth, that they are my own invention, and I have made plenty of

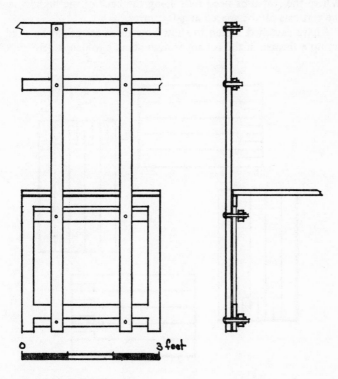

31. Detail of handrail structure.

them. It is quite sensible to paint the horizontal rails white, the clamping pieces black, leaving the verticals natural. Don't be tempted by the attractions of more elaborate handrails that need sockets fitted to the sides of the rostrums, as this will mean that these rostrums are not standard and have to be hunted out for particular placing. On the other hand don't accept my invention if you can think of a better way of solving the problem. You will notice that where the lowest raised level is one step only (i.e. 6 in. or 7 in.) there is no need to put a handrail. At the sides of each set of tiers, the verticals are placed at 1 ft 6 in. centres, two to each rostrum end. Where the rostrums need rails along the back of the highest level, the verticals can be spaced at 3-ft centres.

I have sketched a plan to show how rostrums might be used to set up a theatre in the round, seating about 250 people (the precise

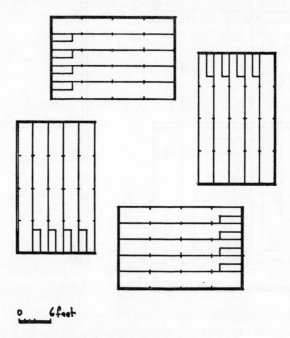

0   6 feet

32. Setting up a theatre in the round with tiers of portable rostrums (no consideration given to limits imposed by the size and shape of the hall).

number will depend on the width of the chairs used), keeping all considerations as straightforward as possible. Eighty standard parallels are used, 16 of each height: 7 in., 1 ft 9 in., 2 ft 11 in., 4 ft 1 in., 5 ft 3 in. Sixteen steps are also required, measuring 4 ft 6 in. × 1 ft 6 in. and 7 in. high. Handrails will be required round three sides of each set of tiers, unless one or more of the blocks is against a wall.

In fact, things are seldom so straightforward when taking over an existing room and converting it into Theatre Two. If the room is fairly small, you will want to set the rostrums against the walls all the way round, but it is unlikely that the doors will be in convenient places. In Scarborough, for instance, the concert room presents not only a doorway problem, but also there are radiators and large heating pipes along three walls, there is an existing platform to be negotiated, one corner of the room is rounded, and, as you might expect, the walls do not measure in multiples of our module; so special fitting pieces have to be devised to fill in the gaps. Corner steps and three tread steps have also been called into being. The first level is 1 ft 2 in., rather than 7 in., because the front row of seats is on floor level. The resulting sketch looks a bit complicated; and it has sometimes been found better to use another room in the Library, the large lecture room, which is in many ways not so suitable as the concert room, but at least requires an easier set-up. For the concert room the schedule of equipment is as follows:

Standard parallels, plan 3 ft × 6 ft
                     height 1 ft 2 in.—19
                          2 ft 4 in.—17
                          3 ft 6 in.—13
Special parallels, cantilevered (to go over radiators), plan 3 ft × 6 ft
                     height 4 ft 8 in.—12
Standard parallels, plan 3 ft × 3 ft
                     height 1 ft 2 in.—1
                          2 ft 4 in.—2
                          3 ft 6 in.—1
Corner steps—8
Single-tread steps—7
Three-tread steps—2
Three sets of handrails
Special fitting pieces (marked S on drawing)
Set of 4-in. blocks on existing platform.

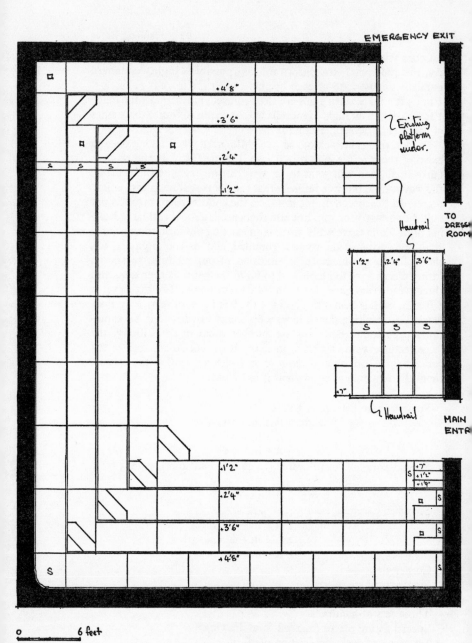

EMERGENCY EXIT

+4'8"

+3'6"

Existing
platform
under.

+2'4"

S   S   S   S

+1'2"

TO
DRESS
ROOM

Handrail

+1'2"   +2'4"   +3'6"

S   S   S

7"

Handrail

MAIN
ENTR

+1'2"

+7"
+1'2"
+1'9"

S

+2'4"

S

+3'6"

S

S

+4'8"

0 ————— 6 feet

33. Tiers of portable rostrums used to set up the Library
Theatre, Scarborough. The hall presents several problems
and a number of special pieces (marked S) have to be added
to the standard units.

The touring schedule of the Studio Theatre company included halls of many different shapes and sizes, and we wanted to carry enough rostrums to take advantage of the largest hall, without exceeding the capacity of our truck, but in some places there might be space to spare, as in the Municipal Hall at Newcastle-under-Lyme. Our step increments were only 1 ft and, because we usually had one or two rows on floor level, again this was the height of the bottom level. Note, too, that we were able to use steps only 3 ft wide —easier to carry but not otherwise recommended. The plan also shows stairways at the back of the tiers. These serve as access ways for both audience and actors.

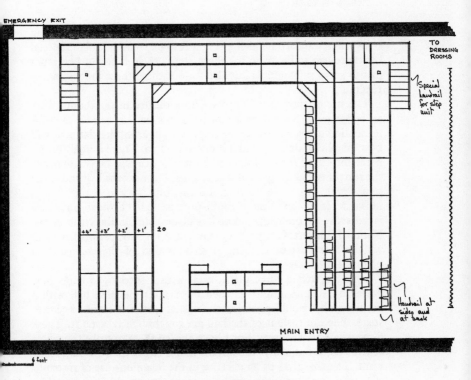

34. Tiers of portable rostrums used to set up a theatre in the round at the Municipal Hall, Newcastle-under-Lyme.

The schedule of rostrums used is as follows:

Standard parallels, plan 3 ft × 6 ft
                    height 1 ft—19
                           2 ft—21
                           3 ft—14
                           4 ft—14
Standard parallels, plan 3 ft × 3 ft
                    height 1 ft—2
                           2 ft—2
                           4 ft—2
Corner steps—4
Single-tread steps—16
Seven-tread steps—2

The seven-tread steps were made up of three units: two three-tread steps and a standard parallel 3 ft × 4 ft in plan and 2 ft high. Special banisters had to be made for these steps, their function being not just to serve as handrails but also to lock these three units securely together.

The use of rostrum units to set up a theatre in the round offers an opportunity for having a multi-purpose hall. It can be used for presenting plays, and, since the stage is on floor level, a flat floor will be available for dancing, exhibitions and so on. There is no difficulty here. But don't forget that good storage space will be required for the rostrums and equipment, and it should be near the hall and at the same level; otherwise moving the rostrums to and fro will be a nuisance. It will be a limited multi-purpose hall, of course, and there is no sense in pretending that it will be suitable for visits of the National Theatre Company on tour, nor for any performances in which an important element is an imitation of the conventional picture-frame stage.

I have sketched three plans, each with a section, to show how portable rostrums might be used for a multi-purpose hall with a flat floor, that would provide a thrust-stage, an end-stage, or centre-stage. The dimensions of the hall are roughly 72 ft × 60 ft. These dimensions are arbitrary, but I have chosen them to make the whole scheme come out easily; though the hall is larger than I would really want. The size gives us an exercise in the ingenious use of rostrums stacked on rostrums; the smaller number that would be required by a smaller hall can easily be worked out.

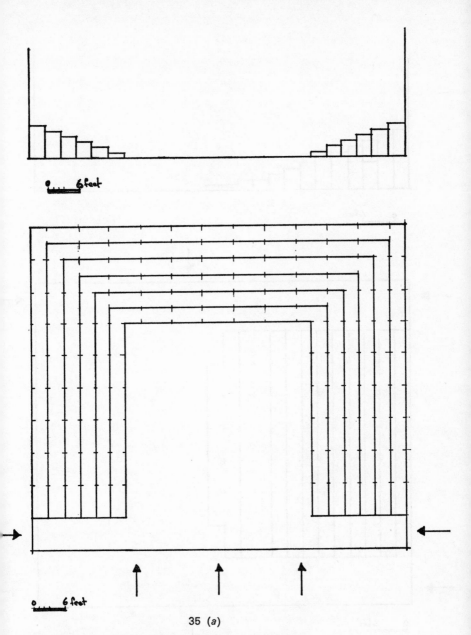

o ⊢⊢⊢⊢⊢ 6 feet

o ⊢⊢⊢⊢⊢ 6 feet

35 (a)

35. A set of portable rostrums could be used to make a modest adaptable theatre, providing: (a) a thrust stage, and, on the next two pages, (b) an end stage and (c) a centre stage.

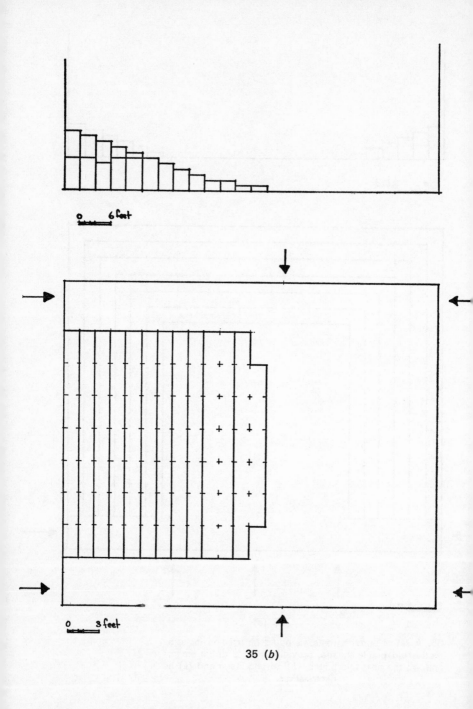

0 ___ 6 feet

0 ___ 3 feet

35 (b)

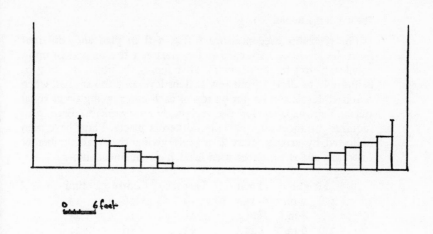

0 ⊢⊢⊢⊢⊢⊢⊣ 6 feet

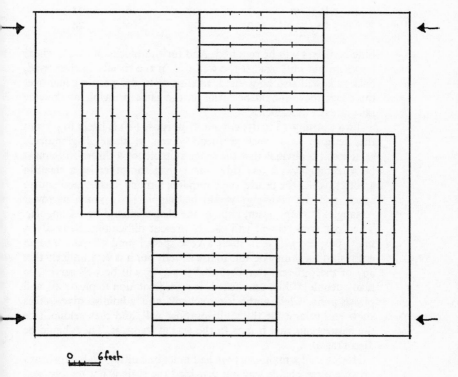

0 ⊢⊢⊢⊢⊢⊢⊣ 6 feet

35 (c)

The rostrums used measure 6 ft × 3 ft in plan and, different from the levels we have used so far, start at 1 ft 2 in. and go up in equal steps to 7 ft; the reason for abandoning the initial step of 7 in. is not only to allow a front row at floor level but also so that, when required, levels can be put on top of each other, going up at equal steps. This happens for the end-stage arrangement. Each plan requires entrances into the hall in different places. These have been indicated by arrows. Here is a table giving the total number of rostrums, and the number used in each arrangement shown:

Height	Total	Thrust	Centre	End
1 ft 2 in.	19	19	16	19
2 ft 4 in.	21	21	16	21
3 ft 6 in.	23	23	16	21
4 ft 8 in.	25	25	16	21
5 ft 10 in.	27	27	16	21
7 ft	29	29	16	24

Side banisters will be required. And for the blocks of levels whose backs do not butt against the walls, as in the theatre in the round, back rails will also be wanted, to stop seats and people going over the edge; these should be made on the same principle as the side rails already described.

Two warnings. Firstly, any multi-purpose hall is likely to present the designer with vast problems. Even in these diagrammatic sketches it is obvious that the space suitable for a thrust-stage must be a rectangle with one side longer than the other by a smallish amount, while the centre-stage requires a much smaller and square space, and the end-stage would be happier in a much narrower rectangle. Perhaps, even, none of the shapes should be rectangular. The door arrangement will clearly present difficulties. Secondly, a multi-purpose hall is in itself a very special kind of space and an enthusiast for it may be able to use it well; but it is very unlikely that any of the different purposes that it serves will be well served, so many people will be unsatisfied. It is an invitation to please all, and please none. Civic authorities, schools and administrative bodies show enthusiasm for the multi-purpose hall, and they seldom face the frustrations that it puts in the way of its users. They should be discouraged.

However, if a multi-purpose hall must be built, portable rostrums provide a reasonable way out provided the scale is not too big, and the standard of finish demanded not too high. Where a larger hall is needed, a multi-purpose hall begins to lose feasibility. Several halls begin to become necessary, and at least one of them should be as large as you like, while another should be small, and might be designed to form one of the theatres with a central stage surrounded by portable rostrums, as described in an earlier version of our Theatre Two.

All these variants on Theatre Two have been temporary conversions. The Victoria Theatre at Stoke is a permanent conversion, the seating rows being raised not on rostrums but on fixed levels. This results in a conversion that more neatly fits the hall (by no means an ideal one for the purpose), but otherwise the arrangement is much the same as we have been dealing with all along. It is yet another version of Theatre Two.

If the hall in which Theatre Two is set up differs in its measurements from the ones we have chosen, little difficulty should be experienced in reworking the plan and getting out the appropriate schedule.

Nothing very difficult has been suggested so far. If the décor of this converted hall is in your hands (that is to say, provided it doesn't belong to a landlord who wants to retain an existing décor, and provided you have the money to buy some paint) make sure that all the walls are finished in dark colours and that paintwork is matt. Emulsion paint is ideal, and International Paints offer some good colours in their House and Garden range of Interlight—Thames Green, Blueberry, or Peacock Blue. Or have your own colours prepared—mauve, blue, deep green, maroon, purple and so on. There are also good wallpapers using these colours. But avoid precise patterns with clean shapes in contrasting colours. The ceiling should also be dark —either blue or black—and painted with a matt finish. These dark shades and the matt finish tend to pick up very little light spill, thus enabling the spotlights to do their job as well as possible when the time comes to concentrate the audience's attention on the acting area. There is no need for dark colours to look dull, and a good designer should be able to devise a very attractive scheme of decoration. If a hall is to be used as a theatre, let us get it to look as attractive and exciting as possible.

It is important that the audience should hear the actors clearly and easily. But acoustics will probably be unkind to a central stage that is set down in a hall never intended for the purpose. Besides, even in brand new buildings, acoustic experts tend to be arbitrary and are often, as far as theatres go, wrong in their predictions. Of course there is no reason why Theatre Two, if we were building anew rather than converting, should not have very good acoustics.* The overall distances between actor and audience are small enough to allow of straightforward acoustic treatment in any theatre in the round; and if in this country we do not have such a theatre, fine examples can certainly be found in the United States. Obviously it is not possible to anticipate the acoustic problems of every hall, but usually the problem is one of too great a reverberation time, due to too large a volume of space. A false ceiling may help here (but it will be expensive)—and the acoustic problem may then be dealt with while dealing with positions for stage lighting. In certain very small halls there may be echoes bouncing across from wall to wall, and these can probably be subdued by putting good sound absorbing panels (of, for instance, expanded polystyrene) on one wall, or two adjacent walls.

Theatre in the round does not make use of conventional stage scenery of the timber frame and canvas sort. But among other things, it will want to take advantage of suspended units; it is easy enough to make provision for this in a new building, and it may sometimes be possible in a converted hall (while dealing with lighting and acoustic problems). In either case the principles are the same. The roof void should be designed so that pulley blocks can be carried and lines provided for suspending over the acting area such things as decorative light fittings (a chandelier, a gas light and so on), abstract objects and realistic pieces (a branch of a tree, a swing, a window frame). At the same time the occasional entrance from above should be allowed for. In many plays such an entrance is reserved for the *deus ex machina*, depending on pulleys, but ladders, ropes and, possibly, wires may be helpful in certain plays. To summarise, the roof void needs to have reasonable head room, a solid floor, safety rails round the troughs, its own illumination, good access and escape ways, and communications with the control room.

From anticipating the needs of conversions, let us now turn to an actual project, planned in 1962 to serve as a Civic Theatre for Newcastle-under-Lyme. The theatre was not in fact built because at that time the government did not think it right for a small borough to spend money on a theatre; the scheme was rejected without the plans even being examined—this was irrelevant. So we missed having a properly built theatre in the round through nothing but the bad

* See J. E. Moore, *Design for Good Acoustics* (Architectural Press).

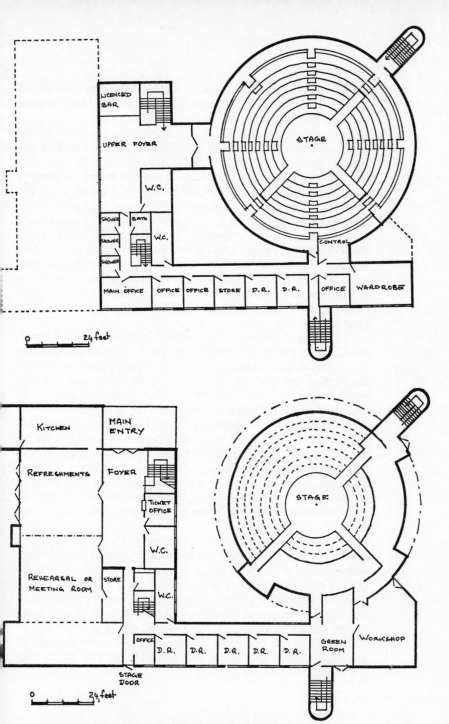

36. Stephen Garrett's designs for the proposed theatre at Newcastle-under-Lyme.

luck of timing (and six months either way might have seen the scheme accepted without trouble). But that's another story. Let me describe the drawings as though the building actually existed.

The architect was asked to design a theatre in the round to seat about 400 people. A second hall was to be designed for functions that require an end-stage. The buildings should be attractive and provide a busy social centre. The architect was told to work to a budget of £60,000. This is a fifth of the price that one might expect to pay for an orthodox theatre. The site chosen was a small public park, called the Brampton. It is a few minutes' walk from the centre of the town, but there is ample space for car parking. The theatre would stand between two existing houses, one of which serves as a museum and the other as an Arts Centre where meeting facilities are provided for local groups devoted to leisure activities. A development scheme for the park had already envisaged the construction of a children's boating pool, which would lie on the south side of the theatre.

The architect conceived the building in three related volumes. First, the theatre in the round itself, circular in plan and standing as a squat cylinder on the site. Second, a rectangular block to take the second hall and the main audience facilities. Third, a connecting wing that would contain dressing rooms and other back-stage accommodation. Approaching from the road, these low-lying shapes would proclaim something unusual, and manifest something of their function. Looking at the drawings, the elevation is simple and straightforward. The central acting area is just above ground level, with gently sloping access to back-stage areas at ground level. The auditorium is steeply sloped in seven stages and an access level, or balcony, surrounds the whole, and is cantilevered beyond the main structure. An overall lighting grid is fixed below the domed roof.

The foyer gives on to a generous stairway. This is the way up to the theatre. The second hall is made up of three areas; a raised stage, with access to the dressing rooms, a small auditorium which can be used as a rehearsal room or lecture room, and a refreshment space, served by an adjacent kitchen. Glass doors open on to a terrace overlooking the boating pool. The rehearsal room and refreshment space can be joined by opening folding doors, giving a larger hall or auditorium for the end-stage. This is obviously a very modest hall and might seat 200 people; it is not intended to accommodate touring companies.

It is, perhaps, worth noting that there is a fully equipped proscenium arch theatre in Hanley, three miles away. It is now no longer
a playhouse but a few years ago it used to be a reasonably good date,
where touring companies, opera and ballet included, performed from
time to time. There is also a fine little theatre with a proscenium
stage at the Mitchell Memorial Hall. However, there is a great deal
of amateur activity in North Staffordshire, and we calculated that
many companies would want to use both the theatre in the round
and the second hall with its end-stage.

Referring again to the drawings, the second hall is designed so
that it can be available for lectures, small concerts, meetings of
various sorts, and as a dance hall and banqueting room. Further,
by making use of the small hall as a rehearsal room during the day,
the company will leave the theatre in the round available whenever
it is preferred for such functions. These activities, together with
eating and drinking, should be, of course, an essential part of a civic
theatre.

As members of the audience come upstairs, a bar and exhibition
space are on the right—and to the left is the entrance to the theatre,
across a bridge. A balcony goes all round the auditorium, and from
this, stairs lead down giving access to the rows of seats. Emergency
exits are provided. A small section of the balcony is taken up by
the control room which will house the control and distribution
boards and sound equipment. The three main actors' entrances are
located under the short access ways.

The acting area itself is a circle of 24 ft diameter. No arrangements
have been made for traps, nor for wing space and entrances that
might allow of scenic boat trucks. A revolving stage has obvious
attractions but has been omitted. The budget does not cover such
things.

The proposed theatre in the round for Newcastle-under-Lyme
generated a good deal of excitement, but since then most of the
people working on the scheme have had more experience, which has
led to fresh ideas. In 1962 we were concerned very much to build
a small theatre on a modest budget, to serve a small audience and
remain economically viable. Theoretically the problem was solved,
but never put to the test.

My main objections to large theatres are two. Firstly, I do not see
the sense in building a large theatre unless there is some evidence
that a large audience is available. In such a place as Newcastle-under-
Lyme all the indications point to a small potential. And the closure

of large theatres in the neighbourhood must be a warning; though it is no proof that a large theatre might not survive since there are so many factors to consider. One may be tempted to assume that the failure of a large theatre must have been due to its old-fashioned form, and to base an argument on the assumption that a central stage reflects more attractively modern ideas than the enclosed stage. But there is no real evidence for this, if only because there has been no trial. However, it needs no great perception to observe that, in general, a playhouse is at present not a very popular place; it is likely to be less popular now than it was fifty years ago. And if we calculate conservatively on this axiom, the case for small theatres in such places as Newcastle-under-Lyme is well-founded. Negatively, if a big theatre is built in spite of such indications, the policy of the company is likely to deteriorate in order to pursue popularity; this may be seen, for instance, at the Theatre Royal in Hanley, which is still open. But it cannot be kept open economically as a playhouse. To pay its way the theatre now houses bingo. Of course, even a small playhouse can fail to attract enough people; it, too, may turn to bingo or whatever happens, at the time, to be popular entertainment. The long history of the theatre is filled by such changes, and few are the playhouses that have held steadfastly to any one policy for more than a dozen years together. But if a small playhouse fails after the failure of a large playhouse, we can suspect that not even a minority of the neighbouring public has any interest in plays at all. Our suspicions are still not proofs. The reasons for both failures may lie elsewhere. Perhaps the large playhouse was draughty and had poor acoustics, while the small one put on performances of such a low standard that no one could enjoy them. In our present argument there must be a tacit assumption that such things are as well looked after as they should be. All things being equal. . . . It is probably true that a small theatre with a particular policy ought to be able to maintain that policy more easily than a large theatre.

My second main objection to large theatres is more practical. In most large theatres too many people in the audience are too far away from the actors; too many of them cannot see properly the action on the stage, nor can they hear what is said by the actors. This should not necessarily be attributed to bad speaking by present-day actors; though old theatre-goers may jump to such a conclusion. I recently heard a distinguished theatre critic, who wore a deaf-aid, reprove modern actors for poor speech, at a public lecture; a member of the audience, who also wore a deaf-aid, stood up at question-time to applaud the point and to add his own experience, since he had seen many plays at the Lyceum in which Irving had performed and had been unable to hear a good half of what that great actor said; lesser actors were entirely inaudible. Things are not like that nowadays. . . . The fact is that in many theatres, seating a thousand or more people, from many seats you can hear a play easily and from some you will miss entirely much of the dialogue. Amplifying the sound through microphones and loudspeakers usually destroys the living quality of the voice, and, apart from certain intrinsic difficulties of a technical nature, it destroys much of the advantage that a theatre may have over television. In programmes that marked the opening of new theatres at the turn of the century, a boast was often printed that the stage can be seen from every part of the house. The fact that the boast needed to be made at all arouses one's suspicions. Some of these theatres are still unaltered and we can test the claim. It is severely accurate. The stage can be seen. But from many seats only a small proportion of the stage; and certainly not enough of it to allow one to enjoy a play. What the boast really meant, perhaps, in those days, was that if you pay enough for your seat you will see and hear perfectly, but if you buy the cheaper tickets you belong to the class that doesn't matter anyhow! The effect of a large play-house on acting technique I examine on page 70. Certainly, both from the actor's and the audience's point of view, then, I consider the large playhouse to be destructive.

Both my objections are limited. If there clearly is a demand for a large playhouse because there is clearly a large potential audience, then why not build one, provided also the disadvantages inherent in large playhouses can be overcome? Well, can the disadvantages be overcome? Yes. The moment the stage comes out from behind the picture frame, the moment it becomes an open as opposed to an enclosed stage, more people can be wrapped round the stage without increasing the distance they must be from the stage. The figures given on page 71 show this conclusively. But those figures are based on actual examples, and no-one has yet taken the theatre in the round to a logical conclusion in this respect. I now propose to show how a theatre in the round could be built to satisfy the demand for size while respecting the necessity for proximity and for good sightlines. Acoustics are less capable of demonstration, and all I can say is that there is no reason why the acoustics should not be perfect.

Before outlining the theatre, we can build up its importance by noting that many people object to the centre stage because it is always on such a modest scale. Richard Southern says:

> So far as experiments with theatres in the round have gone today in France, Italy, the United States, Great Britain and elsewhere, it would seem that they have all had to be limited to small theatres seating comparatively small audiences. . . . Now there are certain economic factors at work in the professional theatre, and one outstanding is that you must have a big enough audience to make your show pay, or you must close down—or be subsidized. For all ordinary purposes of professional theatre work, a paying audience needs to be of the order of 600 or 800 people before even the prospect of covering costs from popularly priced seats becomes a fair one. If the audience can be raised to 1000, so much the better. . . .*

Several of the facts here can be refuted or debated; for instance, by no means *all* examples of theatre in the round are small, and I have already drawn attention to the Casa Mañana in Fort Worth, and there are many more than a dozen Music Tents with centre stages all over the United States, and they usually seat over a thousand people round a centre stage. And one wonders why a theatre in the round must be tested against commercial accountancy when so few important theatres have ever survived without subsidy; and if most of the provincial repertory theatres in this country are subsidised, why should we demand that a theatre in the round must prove that it can do without before we even consider it? This is cavilling. The point behind Southern's remarks remains valid, but he states:

> It seems that if the ring of seats reaches above five or six rows deep (say between 200 and 300 people), there will be difficulties in hearing, because the actors must always speak with their backs to some of the audience.

I believe that careful design can overcome the acoustic problem, provided the person in the audience is not rendered deaf by the thickness of his own prejudice against actors' backs. However, I won't stretch Southern's limits too far (it is not in my own interest to do so, since I want the audience close to the stage), and I will get an audience of a thousand.

In the plan that we are going to look at I have kept the whole

* Richard Southern, *The Medieval Theatre in the Round* (Faber & Faber).

scheme as simple as possible, and have made my calculations very approximately. The circular stage has a diameter of 18 ft. There are three access gangways at stage level for the actors (which can also be used as exit-ways by the audience), and three stepped access ways for the audience to the seating rows (though these ways can also be used by the actors). There are seven rows in the main circles of seating, but behind the last row I have put a standing space; and the last row and its standing space have been added overhead on two balcony levels. Here are the figures that show, roughly, how the accommodation grows with each succeeding row:

Row	Number of people	Accumulated total
1	30	
2	42	72
3	54	126
4	66	192
5	78	270
6	90	360
7	102	462
Standing	110	572
First gallery	214	786
Second gallery	214	1,000

The overall diameter of the theatre has now reached 66 ft, but we have not considered stairways and all the various spaces that must be related to the stage and the auditorium. As I have sketched the plans, no one in the audience of 1,000 need be more than 24 ft from the stage.

But there are two questionable points about this idea. Firstly, the tendency in theatre design has recently been against putting the audience on different levels, mainly because the balconies and galleries of a conventional theatre have become identified with a social distinction between classes. But a glimpse at the drawing board makes little sense of this objection in the present example. A more concrete objection to the galleries of large theatres is that the seats are too far away from the stage, and this is certainly not so in our case. Secondly, standing room in a theatre is not usually acceptable; but I feel that where a play is popular enough to fill all the seats, it is sensible to have an overflow area which yet need not gape emptily when the play is not so popular; and anyhow some people (I am one myself) would often prefer to stand, provided the stage can be easily seen, both because you have freedom of movement to

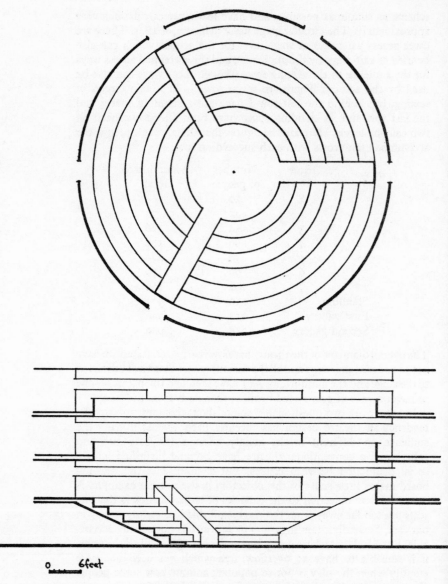

0 ___ 6feet

37. Theatre in the round with a circular plan and two upper
levels for seating.

fidget and because you may only want to see part of the play and then move away without upsetting other people in the audience. But the main reason for having these galleries, and the standing room, is quite simply that a theatre is much more exciting to act in, and to be in, if it is packed with as many people as possible in the volume available. Naked walls are a waste of good, usable space. The only consideration that stops me advocating an audience suspended from the ceiling is that the viewing position would be very uncomfortable and the sightlines more than a little unsatisfactory! But the sketch is practical, sensible and could be used as the starting point for a very exciting theatre.

In the process of developing the idea with an architect I should ask him to consider a slightly more sophisticated plan which, instead of being circular, would be ellipsoid. As it is, architects mostly dislike designing circular structures because of the practical difficulties in building; bricks and lengths of timber are rectangular units, and we measure in straight lines. So a circular building usually causes trouble. I believe this to be a fact. It is a fact that horrifies me and shakes my belief in technological progress, and I refuse to have my imagination, at least, restricted by it. The ellipse, to be sure, will cause even more trouble. The reason for rejecting rectangular and circular plans is this: the rectangle wastes space, and seats at the ends of rows towards the back of the theatre must be awkwardly placed, looking, not at the stage, but across the adjacent bank of seating, while a circle presents us with an acting area unsympathetic to most of the spaces it must stand for. Rooms are rectangular, roads are straight, fields and hillsides are wild. The circle is too precise, with too strong an emphasis on the central point. The American director, Alan Schneider, after much experience of directing plays on the centre stage, came to the conclusion that a circular acting area provided no opportunity to make focal points (other than in the centre), that the shape was amorphous, undynamic, and that an audience would suffer from the kind of listless disorientation that is reputed to make lighthousemen, confined too long in their circular rooms, go mad. The elliptical plan that I want is of a special sort, and I came across it while trying to solve a perennial problem. The problem: how best to put a theatre in the round into an existing rectangular hall. For a touring company, going into halls of different sizes, the answer had to be a rectangular plan, made of rectangular units. A permanent conversion may give an opportunity for a circular structure, but a good deal of space is wasted. Now the necessity to reconcile circular and linear motions and shapes had been fully explored by the Danish inventor, Piet Hein, and he has devised a formula for what he calls a superellipse that comes, as it were, half way between a circle and a square, or between an ordinary ellipse and the rectangle that contains it. The shape is very attractive, and can provide the outline for roundabouts at traffic intersections (as proposed in Stockholm), or for the three-dimensional supereggs that decorate shelves all over Scandinavia.*

While working on superelliptical shapes for a converted theatre, they began to grow into my thinking. And I would like to use this shape for the plan of a theatre in the round. And possibly for the section too. But now I am beginning to escape entirely from financial

* Martin Gardner, *Mathematical Games* (Scientific American, Sept. 1965).

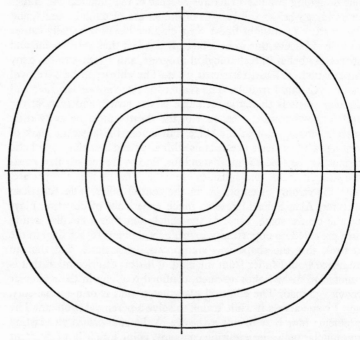

38. The superellipse, devised by Piet Hein, is an ideal compromise between rectangle and ellipse; it therefore suggests a solution to the problem of adapting a rectangular hall for theatre in the round.

restrictions, and my imagination is constructing an absolute gem of a theatre.

A slightly more prosaic but, in its way, I hope, still exciting theatre that would also be interesting to work in is my Fish and Chip Theatre, originally conceived for Scarborough. The architect's brief is to build a theatre in the round, accommodating about 400 people. In addition to the information given for Theatre Two, our special requirements include a rectangular stage that, taken as datum level, has rising seating rows on two sides, a low standing room pit on the third side, and a dining room level on the fourth. All around the theatre, at (or above) the level of the back row, there is a viewing bar, arranged so that you can sit for a drink and snack and watch the play at the same time. Kitchens and serveries and bars to be provided, offering a limited range of refreshments, including fish and chips, soup and rolls, salad bowls, buns, cakes, biscuits, fruit, nuts, ice-cream, beer, coffee, tea, soft-drinks, and wines. Serve yourself at the counter. All sections of the auditorium should be organically connected to encourage free flow of audience from one place to another, even during the performance. The design should be asymmetrical, and invite movement. The seats should be generously spaced. Proportions so related to human stature that the actors and audience dominate the building and not the other way round.

Noise problems? Yes, but the science of acoustics exists and can cope with everything we are likely to demand. Floor, wall and ceiling treatments must be sensibly chosen. The viewing bar should be a good rowdy place, and therefore acoustically separated from the main auditorium with viewing facilities through a restricted opening —and sound reinforcement from the stage through a series of loudspeakers, locally controlled; plug jacks for headphones which may help deaf people and the occasional attentive person on a particularly noisy pay-day performance.

The stage should be provided with traps, an orchestra pit and a balcony acting area. Comfortable dressing rooms with showers and divans for resting: the actors will need them.

In planning administrative offices and technical facilities, provide for a production policy that will present straight plays (from Aeschylus to Becket, Aristophanes to Coward, by way of Shakespeare, Molière and the latest West End success, to every new play that shows a trace of talent for entertaining an audience), musical shows, ballet—and probably, therefore, what amounts to three

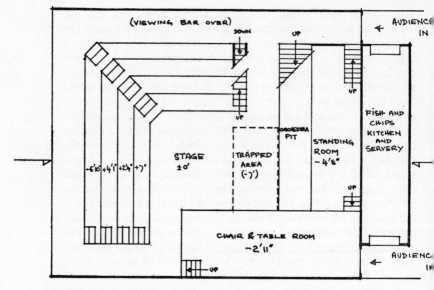

GROUNDFLOOR PLAN

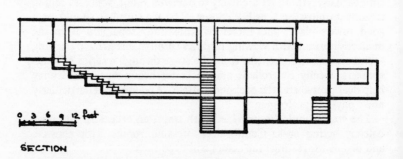

0   3   6   9   12 feet

SECTION

39. Rough plan and section of the Fish and Chip Theatre.

9. The Victoria Theatre at Stoke-on-Trent. (*Photo Ian Stone.*)

10. "Turn Right at the Crossroads", the first Sunday club performance at 41 Fitzroy Square, London.

11. "The Man of Destiny", presented at the Library Theatre in Scarborough.

12. "Usher", Elizabeth Bell in a performance at Scarborough. (*Photo Norman Gold.*)

13. Teatro Sant' Erasmo in Milan.

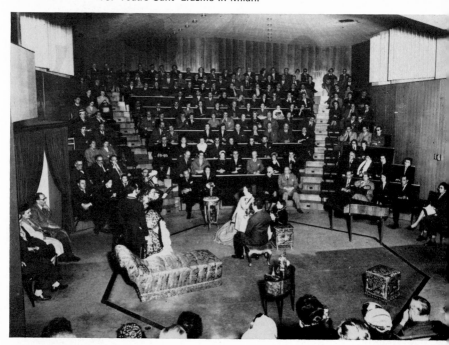

companies at once; but here sometimes working together, for, say, *The Beggar's Opera* or our revue, and sometimes splitting for morning, afternoon and evening shows, for touring, or for holidays; also, of course, plan for fashion shows, mannequin parades and hairdressing demonstrations, cookery demonstrations, trade shows, including machinery and gadget sessions; concerts, particularly of jazz and chamber music; poetry recitals, political meetings, ping-pong tournaments; dances, dinners, doings and happenings, and such other hilarities as may from time to time be devised for the delight and entertainment of people by people. Ensure that a car can be got on to the stage. Provide for power required for, say, a welding demonstration or freezing the floor for an ice-show. Be generous with toilet facilities and rest rooms. Provide a first-aid room. Anticipate television transmission (control room probably an OB unit, but camera positions and adjacent wiring must be provided). Plan generous wardrobe room and storage.

Architects will probably notice that although we are here primarily concerned with theatre in the round as a form of playhouse, the actual arrangement of a central acting area with a surrounding audience is a common one, particularly in sport. The cockpit, the bull ring and the football stadium have this pattern. Wimbledon, Wembley and the Oval offer formal examples. The many parallels between drama and sport justify our noting two things; one, that the arrangement is, to understate the case, satisfactory, and few people complain at seeing the back of a football player. Nor does the player develop the technique of gyration. Movement is part and parcel of his play. Two, that no special education is necessary for your sports spectator, nor is he a representative of a peculiar minority. Before drawing conclusions that relate to the theatre, attention should be paid to certain differences between sport and drama. Among the most tangible differences is the fact that actors speak, that vocal skill is exhibited in the theatre. A lecture hall certainly must offer a linear relationship between speaker and audience, and, I daresay, some people may think the drama is nearer to lecture than to sport. I don't. In my opinion drama is primarily action, and speech is mainly justified as an adjunct to action. But the issue is a more complicated one than this, and the size of the arena and amphitheatre must be considered. There does seem immediate justification for strengthening our conviction that theatre in the round only seems odd or unusual to those people who have already accepted a limited notion of what a theatre should be; a notion, incidentally, that may itself

E

turn out to have been odd and unexpected when the time comes to write a long history of the theatre.

The entertainment that most nearly bridges the gap between drama and sport, also makes notable use of the central acting area is circus. Here, though, the argument is complicated by the entry of animals. I have often been amused by the fact that the Opera House in Scarborough used to be a circus, and the stage can still be approached via the elephant walk.

In this connection, music also has parallels with drama. Of the arts, these two take time. And the manipulation of time can be observed from all round. The very fact the time is being manipulated can, perhaps, best be observed when there is a surrounding audience and when no mere look and look again can recapture the same picture. Unfortunately, the picture-frame stage has imposed not only on the drama but also on music; it is interesting that the art of moving pictures is now moving away from the containing frame, and cinema architecture now seems anxious to disguise its limited view while the theatre is desperately clinging to the frame as though its life depended on it. Musicians are practical people and play where they can. But not only is the proscenium arch of little help to them (and more often that not it is a positive hindrance), there is also some indication that chamber music and jazz benefit from both a wholly surrounding audience and the logical arrangement of the players themselves facing inwards towards each other. The new Berlin Philharmonic Hall which has a central concert platform, is likely to have a profound effect on music and concert-going.

It is interesting that opera and dance have, to a great extent, become identified with one form of staging. Certainly classical opera and classical ballet hardly belong in a theatre in the round. They could be done, but procrustean tactics would have to be employed. However, dance and song do not begin and end with certain classics, and there is every reason to suppose that they can fill a central acting area now as well as they did before classical opera and ballet existed. Folk dancing is almost universally watched by a surrounding audience. Both the British Dance Drama Theatre and the Western Theatre ballet have used theatre in the round. And the American Music Tents have at least put musical comedy in the middle of the audience. Clearly, further developments are possible.

In discussing the size of a theatre, enough has probably been said to suggest that practical and theoretical considerations are closely mixed. It is important that the actors should easily be seen and heard, and it is important that the actors should be able to achieve a more or less homogeneous effect on their audience. Further technical demands have been made, that the acting area should have the lowest floor level and not be on a raised platform, and that scenery should not be used. These demands have interesting theoretical justification as well as practical advantages.

Much of the claim for attention made by the central stage must rest in its suitability for modern acting and modern plays, no matter if historical evidence is also called on. Consider, first the raised stage. It puts the actors *above* the audience; it gives them an authority, and puts the audience in an *inferior* position. The actors *look down* on the audience, which *looks up* at the actors. This literal description of the situation is loaded with deeper meaning. The raised stage is ideal for Kings and Heroes, exalted characters, the protagonists of classical and romantic drama. But modern drama has very different protagonists. I suggest that they are usually *on the same level* as the audience which may properly look down on them. Now, secondly, recall that, on a central stage, the actors are seen against a background of audience. They do not have the surroundings of illusion, of painted rooms, or colourful or atmospheric scenery. Instead, they are positively human beings, set against a background of human beings, and against this background each member of the audience will judge their actions. And each member of the audience is part of the background, each sharing responsibility for the action. It seems to me that this relationship between actor and audience reflects very accurately what so many of today's playwrights are striving to achieve. Further, it is a relationship that puts old plays into a new focus. What happens when Hamlet or King Lear forsakes the commanding platform and comes down to our level? We judge them as though they were men like ourselves, we sympathise with them, despise them, love them: surely not entirely against their creator's wishes?

When the play is thus set down in the middle of the audience a further possibility arises. Not only do the characters enter the audience's world more easily, but the audience is more heavily involved, both in the entertainment and in the action of the play, at least to the extent of engagement in the decisions that push the action forward. In this way it is just possible to conceive the idea of a theatre that increases our sensitivity to moral responsibility and exercises our little-used power of choice; this may happen in either of two ways. Firstly, each member of the audience becomes concerned with the play, and uses his powers of volition on behalf of the characters in the play and accepts responsibility for the actions of the characters. I believe this happens more or less in any play. It happens a little when we watch a television play, and a good deal more when the living actors are before us on the stage; and it happens most of all when the audience is close to the actors and when the audience has the actors in a complete embrace. Secondly, though I do not now speak from experience or observation but only from theory, in a theatre where the actors are not tied at all rigidly to the words written by the playwright, but instead have arranged to improvise as much as possible, then choice, at least by the actors, is really being made; and no actor who has played in a theatre in the round with an enthusiastic audience will question that his choice would be greatly influenced by the audience. To exercise this power of choice, to engage our will power, is an important function of the theatre; for these activities are too much hindered during most of our lives and, since they are an essential part of human nature, we are so far robbed of our humanity. Here in the theatre, it seems to me, we can make some preparation to deal with real problems of existence. We find in all great works of art a reflection of life that helps us to see life itself more clearly. This was in Shelley's mind when he called poets the unacknowledged legislators of the world. In a great theatre it is possible that actors and audience can share the greatest of insights and experiences.

8
Production

THEATRE in the round obviously imposes new demands on actors, playwrights and producers. We can take for granted the fact that there will also be much in common with conventional and familiar practice, and there is no need to examine every aspect of it. But there are certain inescapable artistic opportunities and limitations that must be acknowledged.

During rehearsals where should the producer sit? It doesn't matter. There is certainly no need for him to move around the acting area. He should be aware that his acting area is a three-dimensional volume; it has a sculptural impact, and performance adds the dimension of time, giving the audience a view into a complete space–time continuum. These heady words simply draw attention to the blatant fact that most producers are used to composing a picture behind a frame, and that the situation on a central stage is sculptural; but provided he has no preconceived notions of flat moving pictures, the producer will find few problems in the round. Life is the great model that we are striving to imitate and the spatial dimensions of theatre in the round provide a perfectly apt containment for our creation. As far as production is concerned the central stage seems to me to demand fewer conventions. It is therefore difficult to be positive about production in theatre in the round, except to say that it is marvellously exciting to watch actors evolving patterns of movement to illustrate the play within the space at their disposal.

In spite of my own predilection towards creative acting, I'm sure it is perfectly possible for a producer to come to the first rehearsal with a complete *regiebuch*, containing a precise ground plan and every move worked out. The producer who does this must first simply develop the capacity to see the whole action in his mind's eye; there is no insuperable problem. My objection to this procedure is personal, rationalised in part by the feeling that to produce thus is to waste a golden opportunity. For it seems to me that when we talk about "holding the mirror up to nature" (as we very often do), most of us tend to think in terms of the play as being a more or less historical document, providing us with a guide to the manners and customs, the characters and values, of its particular time; and what we should think of, I believe, is rather that the whole theatre mirrors its own age. Every aspect of the theatre, not just the play, reflects our behaviour, and it can be seen as a microcosm of our particular universe. And to my way of thinking, we are presented in the theatre with an ever-fresh opportunity to choose what shall be mirrored. The business of rehearsing a play is an exercise in social behaviour. It gives us, as actors and artists, the chance of forming a group of people who can get to know each other fairly well, and work in an atmosphere of equality, giving and taking, each according to his talent and according to the requirements of the particular performance in view. Further, this group should be sensitive to the needs of society, to the manners and imaginations of the community; here the artists should find their source material—the dramatist for his play, the actor for his performance. The producer's job, then, is to pay attention to all the many technical matters that help the actor in his performance. He should co-ordinate the diverse elements of costume and stage lighting, of publicity and working schedules, and above all he should promote this team-work and this special relationship between actors and audience. And the special relationship between actors and audience in theatre in the round seems to reflect this give and take very strongly; for the audience wraps round the acting area in a metaphorical embrace—good word, for at its best surely the performance of a play is a passionate affair between actors and audience?

Whether he prepares a detailed prompt copy before rehearsals begin, or goes open-minded (and idealistically inspired?) to meet his actors, clearly the producer must have some notion of how to help them. And although the next chapter deals with acting, much of what follows can be considered either as the producer's or the actor's business.

The producer's main task is to feel his way into a fresh relationship with his actors. If he makes a success of this, he will get good performances from them. Between this and conventional production it is a question of balances, slight shifts of emphasis, some of which are obvious and some so subtle as to defy cold print. But I shall list them as well as I can.

It is often assumed that actors in the round must make a lot of moves, the implication being that these have to be, in an artificial sense, devised so that the actor can face all sections of his audience with reasonable frequency. And it is true that you can see performances in which there is excessive and meaningless movement. Such performances are at fault. In fact, a central stage does not necessitate a single meaningless move from any actor. How then does the actor convey his performance all round? The answer is not simple. First, recollect that we have all along stipulated a small theatre. Everyone in the audience is near enough to detect the slightest movement and to interpret the smallest change of expression. The actor has at his command what is almost a new vocabulary of subtle gestures. His least expression is crystal clear to the audience, his motives and intentions are transparent even through his very back. I have replaced a theoretical bad actor with a good one and, in providing him with that new vocabulary, have to some extent contradicted myself. I admit, then, that extra movement is used, though not the excessive and meaningless movement that everyone must object to. Further, there are few moments (in few plays) when a single actor is alone on the stage, and it is important to note that, on a central stage, action and reaction are both important. The audience watches both characters in a duologue. The central stage can hardly provide an upstage or other dominant position, and the smallness of the stage enables the audience to take in both characters. The vague novelty of this situation can be slightly illustrated by noting that young actors playing subsidiary parts in a play on a proscenium stage must frequently be told to keep still, while on a central stage, at worst, they must be told to react with more truth or conviction, and more positively. However, it is true that movement includes stillness. Alan Ayckbourn after half a dozen years of experience in the round, discovered a tremendous power in complete stillness, held, as in a splendid performance of More in Bolt's *A Man for All Seasons*, against a surrounding bustle and movement from other characters. Another good example of stillness came from Stanley Page, performing the part of Doctor Rank in Ibsen's *A Doll's House*. But in each case a special effect was sought, and achieved. Movement or stillness must be selected for good reasons.

The pattern of movement on a central stage can be woven from the various familiar strands of purposeful or utility moves (going to sit down, fetching the matches and so on), movement expressing relationships (going towards the girl friend, moving away from the hated person and so on), and movement directed towards creating a pleasant, or powerful, or amusing design (a circuitous, dance-like pursuit in a love scene, murderers converging on a victim, the husband retreating from his overbearing mother-in-law). There is nothing new here, merely the omission of any thought of a linear projection. Let me explain what I mean by this. On a picture-frame stage, as also on an end-stage or thrust-stage, the actor can note the extreme edges of the block of people who form his audience, or even the boundaries that define the mass of seats in the theatre. He observes these edges in a more or less wide angle of vision that can be bisected to provide a central line. There will naturally be a tendency for the actor to pay attention to this line and to project his performance, not necessarily straight along it, but so that it forms a mean direction in which the performance must go. Such a linear projection affects not just the individual actor, but any two actors—

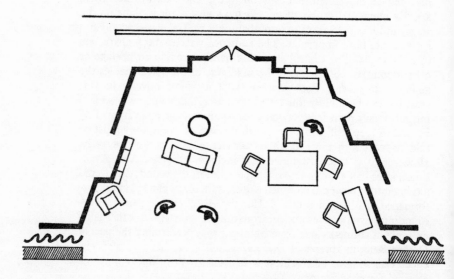

40. Bird's-eye view of stage and actors set for linear projection on a picture-frame stage. (*Drawn by John Jones.*)

who usually arrange themselves (or are arranged by the producer) to face at least a little to the *front*; that is to say, there is a tendency for actors to face their audience and to group along a line more or less at right angles to this line of projection. In theatre in the round, obviously none of this can apply. Both grouping and movement must be seen from all sides to carry their full significance; the event must be plain for all to see, whether it is the husband retreating from the mother-in-law, or the youngsters engaged in the delicate pursuits of love.

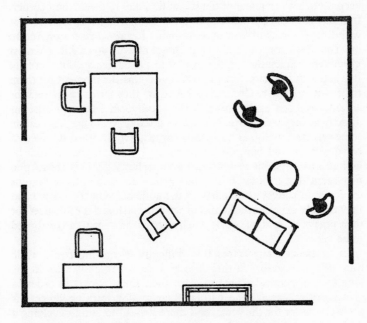

41. Bird's-eye view of stage and actors set for all round projection on a central stage. (*Drawn by John Jones.*)

Relationships assume great power on a small central stage; patterns of movement and stillness become revelationary, and the distances between characters are always dynamic, emphasised by the attitude or line of each person. Finally, any position on the stage can be charged with significance at the actor's choice. There is no intrinsic position of domination, centre stage or anywhere else. Any part of the stage is capable of supporting whatever emphasis the actors put on it. Enter the King; he goes to the centre of the stage to command. Or enter the King; he crosses the stage to the farthest side and turns to command. Again, enter the thief, slyly; he shuffles to centre stage, looks round slowly, frightened. Or enter the thief, keeping to the perimeter of the stage; he sidles to the farthest corner, frightened. Is the character upright, or bent or twisted, expansive or withdrawn? Quick or slow in movement? Legato or staccato? And so on. You, the actor, can make your choice of what you think will most effectively convey the required point to the audience. But there are two actors; two characters in love, say; is this the moment for them to be close together? Or far apart? And are they facing each other for an entirely open exchange (yes, they really can face each other as directly as they want) or is he slightly sideways on to her, concealing some secret? Finally, as her hands come gently forward in token of her desire to hold him, does he walk away, or can you see that he hesitates to admit his real feelings even to himself? This abstraction may seem thin enough, but in fact actors need do nothing false or excessive to convey their parts to the audience. On the other hand they usually experience the discovery of a fresh series of devices for their purposes. And, of course, such devices can be ignored or abused to bad effect.

In rehearsal many actors find difficulty in moving freely while they still have scripts in their hands. I do not think it wise, in the long run, to persuade them to learn their lines quickly in order to give more rehearsal time without books. The learning process is probably easier for the actor, and more helpful to him in evolving a performance, if words and movement are worked on and memorised together. From the earliest rehearsals the actor should be encouraged to respond to written words not only by making sounds but by also making movements. After a number of productions in which this procedure has been followed an actor ought to be able to sight-read a good play, making sense of it vocally and in motion. A producer facing a central stage would be wise to consider this long-term aim, and to encourage his actors to do what they may consider at first an impossibility. It is not an impossibility, as they will discover to their great joy. The producer now finds that this joy helps to initiate meaningful and fluid movement patterns. Acting in the round, will soon, then, be achieved.

Entrances and exits should be made cleanly, observing the logic of the acting area and the style of the play. If the scene is meant to be a room, the actor entering should respond as though coming into a room in spite of the fact that he may be able to see the room and the people in it as he approaches. In a realistic play there does not seem to be any sense in "miming" doors, when so little else that is important to the action has to be mimed; the same applies to windows, which should be taken for granted and not mimed. By all means pour extra light on to the stage to indicate the sun shining into the room, and let the actors respond to this—and the distant view; but there is no need to part imaginary curtains (this belongs of course, to an altogether whimsical production). The room discipline applies in some degree to all entrances; I like the actors to approach the acting area in a more or less normal or negative way and to reach character-isation or performance only when they actually reach the stage. To take a few extreme cases, a slow walking character with a pronounced limp might well make most of his approach swiftly and unhalting. If he were to limp and grunt all the way along the accessway he would take attention off the acting area where it should focus until his entry; a character who runs off laughing loudly should begin to lose his laugh as soon as he leaves the stage and slow down at least enough not to cause a disturbance at the back of the audience.

Entrances and exits are helped if the acting area is well lit, while the surrounding audience is left comparatively in the dark. In fact a surprise entrance can easily be achieved by the sensible use of light—and stillness. A young girl stands reading a letter, lit by a few spot-lights only; by making a swift and quiet approach an actor can sud-denly break into the lit area and surprise both the girl and the watch-ing audience.

We had to solve a problem of this kind in a production of *Hamlet*; the hiding of Polonius behind the arras, in the Queen's closet. Light-ing defined the areas. Half the stage was lit, and here the Queen had her first dialogue with Polonius, who, on Hamlet's approach, crossed over on to the shadowy side of the stage. Hamlet entered and moved straight to the Queen; we thus had a clear picture of the distance to the doorway. When Polonius is discovered he runs down the dark-ness, Hamlet virtually keeping pace with him on the lit side of the supposed arras; finally Polonius makes a rush for the doorway and in doing so runs on to Hamlet's sword. This movement gave the audience an excitement in performance that was audibly breathtaking, and completely lived up to our expectations.

I have always found crowd scenes difficult to stage in the round. A short crowd scene (no matter how many extras may be involved) is no problem; but if six or more characters hold the stage for a whole act they may give trouble. It is, of course, simply a question of masking. I have worked, in the main, with a small company and this point, because of my inexperience with it, may trouble me more than it need. I saw a highly successful production of *Inherit the Wind* at the Pembroke Theatre, and it is a play I would have funked myself. In fact very few plays do crowd the stage for more than a few moments at a time. And a crowd is easy to deal with when someone is dominating the stage, as in a Greek play with its protagonist and chorus. (It is worth saying at once that the Greek chorus becomes wonderfully dynamic in the midst of a surrounding audience; dance and movement patterns acquire a special significance.) The solution to the problem of masking depends sometimes on movement and sometimes on having the characters at different levels, with the help of rostrums or by standing, sitting, kneeling, lying down and so on.

But let us now examine the production scheme of a particular play. *In Camera*, translated from Sartre's *Huis Clos*, is a fascinating play, savage and sophisticated, fantastic yet intensely real, and brilliant in its taut structure. Three people find themselves in a room, with no window. The door is locked from the outside until they decide to stay inside when it opens of its own accord. The furniture is fixed. It cannot be moved. Each of these people is attracted to another and repelled by the third, in patterned relationships, so that each hates the one who offers love—the smart woman desires the journalist who wants the lesbian who craves the smart woman, who hates her while she in turn despises the journalist, who, of course, loathes his pursuer. Each is the tormentor of the other two. This is a hell where we inflict our own punishments on ourselves. There is no need of devils. The play has been produced many times. A producer preparing a ground plan for the play may quickly perceive the necessity for three chairs or settees. They are clearly referred to in the dialogue and necessary to the action. And he might, with a picture-frame stage in mind, arrange them to give a proscenium theatre audience the most satisfactory view of the characters when each is occupied.

Linear projection dictates fairly precisely how this must be done. But a theatre in the round immediately offers the opportunity for arranging three chairs equally spaced round the circumference of a circle and facing inwards. Such an arrangement expresses precisely the relationships between the characters. It would be highly unsuited to the picture-frame stage. The circular plan of the furniture also goes hand in hand with the general movement pattern that arises organically from the text and from the basic idea of the play—each character pursues and is pursued, flees and is fled from in a never-ending, tormented circle. Having seen the play performed in this way I do not understand how it can be better done any other way. Yet I doubt if the playwright, when he wrote the play, had even heard of theatre in the round.

Having accepted the aptness of theatre in the round for this play a producer must also face certain minor problems. There is the business with the door; each of the characters comes into the room, ushered by a flunkey, and then the door closes. Later, after an intense scene, Garcin decides to leave, rushes to the door which he finds locked. He is supposed to beat on the door. Barry Boys, playing this part, fell to his knees and beat on the floor, a beseeching figure—and an adequate substitute for the action suggested in the stage directions. The bell is a problem. Where can you put a bell push or a bell pull on a central stage? The solution in this production had the uneasy air of a makeshift; a bell push was secured to the table that carried the only important movable property in the play (the dagger-like paper knife) and the heavy piece of sculpture that Garcin tries to move and cannot. The furniture, too, being immovable, makes slightly less the unlikelihood of a bell push on a table. But, in the end, it is a small problem, unlikely to upset the play.

Huis Clos has a claustrophobic atmosphere, and it is easy to get this effect on a central stage; the audience will feel it if the actors create it. Stage lighting probably helps, too, if the light is concentrated on the acting area, and the spill into the audience kept to a minimum. In the particular production we have been discussing, the centre of the "vicious circle" was marked by a circular, white rug, and six spotlights from all round were focused down hard on to the rug from the outer grid, striking the floor at an angle of about 45°. The direct light was therefore useful for lighting the actors, and the refracted light came up helpfully from below. An unexpected effect was apparent; each of the sequences where a character looks into the living world, as in a dream, was played with the character standing on this mat which was otherwise never touched, and the actor standing here appeared to be suspended over a luminous void.

Other plays with a more or less claustrophobic atmosphere, such as *The Birthday Party*, *The Caretaker*, *Miss Julie*, *Endgame*, and *Professor Taranne* have worked very well on the central stage, and I suspect it is more a question of sensible acting than anything to do with the form of theatre since plays needing the feel of open space succeed just as well. In this last category one might include *Wuthering Heights*, *King Lear* and several other classical plays. In one such play, extremes of openness were explored; this was Peter Cheeseman's production of *As You Like It* at the Victoria Theatre. For this, a number of peripheral stages were used: stages round the theatre as well as in the centre. The idea suggesting these stages is in the medieval drawings of the Cornish rounds, with their surrounding mansions; and no one would want to claim originality for bringing medieval staging techniques to Shakespeare's plays since he probably made use of such techniques in his own day, and possibly just this one in just this play, at least when it went on tour. One particular scene was remarkably effective: the meeting of Rosalind, disguised, and Orlando in the forest. Rosalind sees Orlando coming, leaves the central acting area, goes up the gangway steps to behind the audience where she climbs on the backrail, and balances by holding on to the vertical stair-rail (access to the ceiling space), and from there she watches him. In a moment he leaves the central acting area by the opposite gangway, but just before he disappears she hails him. In this small theatre the two actors are now as far apart as they can possibly be. About 60 ft. They call to each other across the distance. There are few theatres in which such a distance can be achieved while still keeping the proportions of a small theatre. But the distance itself was only part of the effect. The acting seemed to create a forest glade, and everyone in the audience could sense that they were in it; and now, slowly Rosalind came down, then Orlando; until at the end of the scene they were only a few inches apart. From:

ROSALIND: Do you hear, forester?
ORLANDO: Very well: what would you?

the scene gradually brings them closer and closer, Rosalind enjoying the freedom given by her disguise, and Orlando speaking truer than he thinks:

ROSALIND: . . . And thus I cured him; and this way will I take upon me to wash your liver as clean as a sound sheep's heart, that there shall not be one spot of love in't.

ORLANDO: I would not be cured, youth.

In the audience we enjoy the pleasant irony and in this production it was nicely presented; the effect was stunningly beautiful.

If most of the plays we present are more or less realistic then we shall want to keep mostly to a well defined acting area, but as lyricism or fantasy begin to break into our repertoire there is an increasing pressure to use the whole theatre with imagination. For David Campton's play *Cock and Bull Story*, written to be staged at the new Nottingham Playhouse, the small acting area at Scarborough was enlarged by the addition of a raised corner stage. The sightlines from all seats were not equally satisfactory, but the flow of action was enjoyed by everyone. At the beginning of this play, use was made of direct address to the audience, and, members of the audience replied willingly. I think this device needs to be used tactfully by the producer, but it certainly can be used.

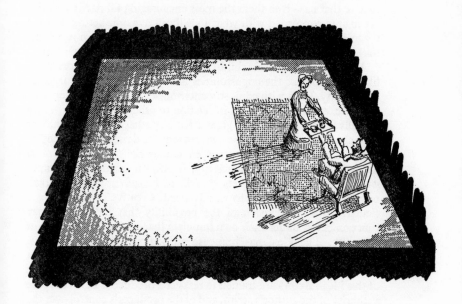

9
Acting

I APPROACH the business of acting with caution. I am not an actor. And I have theories. This is dangerous. And if an experienced actor tells me I'm a fool, I'll respect his opinion. But the theories are still there. I have already made some comments about acting in the last chapter which dealt primarily with production; it is difficult to separate the two. I must admit that I have always enjoyed producing plays, in whatever form of theatre has been available (mostly, therefore, on the picture-frame stage) and my theories about acting have not arisen solely from theatre in the round. However, it is this form of theatre that has given them the most encouraging fillip. My theories are mainly concerned with what I shall call dynamic acting. Let me try to explain what I mean by this—even if my exposition is not entirely clear (as it can hardly be when I am still exploring the idea).

Anyone working with children in the field of creative drama is likely to recognise the opportunities here for education in social responsibility. Even with adult students and actors, improvisation calls for the exercise of discretion in relation to others. At its best, every art calls for choice. And the great artist is, perhaps, the one who not only chooses well but has his own reasons for doing so; both choice and the reason behind it are transcendentally right. As an art, drama depends on group or social activity. It offers us a miniature framework in which certain aspects of civilised behaviour can be worked out, understood and, perhaps, advanced. Creative drama, in particular, gives us a vision of the possibility that individuals may function better under their own impulses than under the guidance of authority. The ideal has immense attractions and, when I have glimpsed it, it has appealed strongly to me. I pursue it. But most work in the professional theatre gives little scope for the emergence of this ideal. Actors are trained to respect a producer's authority, the authority of the author's script, and of the producer's control over the interpretation of the play and over the visual and technical means of presentation. Theatre in the round gives an opportunity for release from at least some of the producer's control. The technical means of presentation can be kept so simple as to interfere not at all with the creative work of the actor. And it may be possible to arrive at an interpretation of the play by common consent.

In fact, even in the most conventional theatre the idea that the producer imposes an interpretation on his actors is often simply false; the actors do their best and that's that. Sometimes the producer's interpretation is clear enough, and, as often as not, it is quite arbitrary and personal and limits the appeal of the performance. Satisfactory performances often arise in spite of the producer whose authority may not always be respected, nor his interpretation understood.

Of course we are still left with the authority of the dramatist's lines. Certainly in a public theatre the script cannot be abandoned without running into trouble with the censor and the licensing authorities. But most actors accept the author's hand as a help and his authority is not usually burdensome. Within these bounds it is possible to stipulate, if not creative drama, at least what might be called creative acting. The producer (or someone else) chooses the play and casts it. The actors work out their movements in rehearsal, set the play, and indicate (if relevant) what special effects of lighting and sound may be required. This, briefly, is a practicable approach to dynamic acting.

When we started the theatre in the round in Scarborough, as manager and producer I had a busy time during rehearsals; management could not be ignored, and the essential obligation I had to the actors was to encourage them, excite them, stimulate their imaginations. And I found that the best time to do this was during morning coffee-break or at lunch or over a pint of beer in the evening. On reflection, I would say that my only important contribution to the company's eventual performances was to ensure that there was always a good coffee-break during rehearsals. Luckily most of the actors in the company responded to this treatment. The performances were as good as we hoped they might be. Perhaps the company was exceptionally brilliant; though I suspect that most actors, in spite of their fears to the contrary, could work creatively together if given the right stimulus, or merely a fair chance.

Actors vary, of course, in their willingness to work out their own production discipline. Some are so used to firm direction that they lose confidence in a production that is even slightly free. Others, after a bewildering and often unwelcome first taste of dynamic acting, soon take to it with enthusiasm. Some actors take to it naturally. But unfortunately most actors, like the rest of us, feel secure when they know where they stand in relation to authority and they prefer more authority to less. Although I believe that less control from the producer should eventually lead to better acting, it obviously requires special circumstances: luck, perhaps, for quick results, or time to establish mutual trust and an awareness of one's own as well as other people's talents. In the commercial theatre, where there is scarcely time to establish even a sense of team-work, let alone artistic ensemble, such notions must remain mostly theoretical, and their development cannot be written about from experience. All the same, without any deliberate effort on our part, theatre in the round does seem to reduce external disciplines on the actor. It is not just that most producers come to theatre in the round more than a little unsure of themselves (though I welcome this, of course, provided they don't compensate for their weakness by superficial displays of strength). There really is less for the producer to do. And much, much more for the actor.

While we are in the process of discovering new conventions, another consideration must be made. Setting can be easily adjusted to the demands of the actors, even if these demands arise (as they probably will) after much rehearsal. An actor creating a role should only be expected to reach an acute sensitivity to his surroundings when the character is fairly firmly established. Producer and designer need not be disturbed by this; indeed it may be helpful to everyone, provided the producer has not made a point of "fixing" the set at the beginning of rehearsal; better to let everyone know that the set is subject to change if experience in rehearsal asks for it. The producer should encourage his actors to move freely during rehearsal. Movements should be tried, discarded, selected, changed or adjusted from rehearsal to rehearsal. Obviously the producer can help the actor by behaving like a representative member of the audience, as it were, applauding what works and expressing doubts at apparent failures in communication.

A question on which actors will almost certainly seek guidance is the degree of "intimacy" required in performance. It is, of course, a beginner's question, taken for granted as soon as satisfactorily dealt with. Many people who advocate the breaking down of the proscenium arch, and speaking against the tyranny of the picture-frame stage, use the word "intimacy" to describe one of the attributes of the promised land on the open stage. I am never quite sure of its meaning in this context. My own concerns are to reduce the physical distance between actors and audience, to put stage and auditorium in one architectural volume, and to ensure that everyone in the audience can see and hear the actors. These mundane demands will lead, I hope, to great enjoyment by the audience of the actors' performances (which, I take for granted, will be skilful and exciting). I am on the defensive when it comes to intimacy of greater scope. It suggests to me two possible dangers; either that the actor will expect a childlike response from his audience (and I'll develop this in a moment) or that the intimacy will be no more than underacting to such a degree that the audience gets little entertainment from the performance. The latter is a real danger. In a small theatre actors are liable to forget they must still project beyond the give and take of the supposed relationships between characters. They are encouraged to this fault by the very conditions of performance. For many plays, for many performances, the actor has probably had small audiences, often fairly undemonstrative audiences, and sometimes audiences that do not fully appreciate the play. The effect of this is to drive the actor in on himself, to make the performance exist solely in its own right. A similar result can come even from the most applauded performance; the actor begins to glow with satisfaction, and subsequently to despise his audience. In each case the actor feels he knows better than his audience and begins to look on performance as being an end in itself without the need to entertain an audience. Finally, the actor leads a very busy life, working an irregular schedule that separates him from his neighbours. Few actors can lead a normal social life. This is a pity, not only because they are thus denied a primary source of artistic material in the observation of other people, but because they are forced to form a closed society of their own. A tremendous amount of work is done by actors and technicians that has little bearing on performance, so separate is the actors' world from the world of the audience. This gives rise to intense performances on stage that mean little to outsiders—to the public. An intimacy to avoid, if it is intimacy at all.

But the intimacy in question is expressly *with* the audience. Isn't that an entirely different thing? Yes, but intimacy between people who know so little of each other as actors know of their audience (and vice versa) is immoral, and likely to be embarrassing to both parties. By all means let us encourage a better acquaintance, shorter working hours for actors (and a more rational use of their time), and all that is thus implied in social responsibility. But this is a long-term policy and usually outside the mere actor's control. It has little to do with the normal traffic of the stage.

I have dodged the issue, to some extent, as can be seen if we look at an amateur performance, where actors and audience can be expected to come from the same community and to know each other. Here we are still likely to find performances so small that they do not fully communicate with the audience. And what should be aimed at here is effective communication.

At a reasonably good performance where communication is effective, people in the audience may feel the impact of a play more strongly in the round (if one could measure such things) than on an enclosed stage. It is common for people at a theatre in the round to be deeply moved, and for them to experience towards the actors feelings that strongly resemble the sensations of real life. If this is intimacy, it is achieved by the actor through strong communication, and calling it into being is a grave responsibility that should be reflected not just in the honesty of performance, but also in the quality and significance of plays chosen for representation.

However, most people's notions of intimacy in acting do not have these serious overtones; they refer to audience participation. We have all heard of the honest jack tar or simple butcher's boy who interrupted some famous actor, playing Macbeth or Othello, to challenge the regicide or to disabuse the Moor. Do we want more of this? No. Such an interruption usually comes from the occasional overwrought moron in the audience; an adult with a child mind. We do not seek it. Such participation in the play belongs to the child audience and it is a special phenomenon that needs skilful handling. Specialists in child drama know how to exercise audience participation, which seems to depend on the inability of children below a certain age to distinguish as precisely as adults between things of imagination and of reality. In his play, *Pinocchio*, Brian Way has his hero swim out to sea; without direct persuasion, children willingly provide the sound of noisy waves for the puppet to swim against. Enter a monster and an awed hush immediately falls; there is no need for the actor to say "Quiet, dears, that's enough sea-noise!" and anyhow few actors could be heard against these oceans. Such a request would be a breach of contract in the imagined world shared between actor and child audience. The solution given arises from a specialist's understanding of the child mind. Children's theatre is of vital importance, not just in the context of professional theatre, but in the whole business of educating civilised human beings. It is a specialised field. Unfortunately the right specialist is a rarer bird than the enthusiast who may love children but can give them no more than poor adult drama.

The differences between children and adults at the theatre must be recognised. Imagination is a precious faculty and it is right that it should be exercised, but there is nothing worthy in persuading adults to behave like children. If anything, the theatre should help children to grow into mature adults, and this might justifiably call for attention.

There is no doubt that there are circumstances when adult participation can work. Plays with a powerful propaganda purpose, such as *Waiting for Lefty*, may indeed actively involve the audience. Stories of Okhlopkov's productions at the Realist Theatre in Moscow reveal the remarkable involvement of the audience. It may work for a community in the process of revolution. But a spectator at Reinhardt's production of *Danton's Death* was merely embarrassed by a neighbour who threw a fit of hysterics—do you withdraw and admire the performance, or smack the lady's face? I saw a performance of Christopher Fry's *A Sleep of Prisoners* in a London church, and the actors advanced up the nave, smelling of greasepaint; here an attempt to establish intimacy between audiences and imaginary characters failed absolutely because, perhaps, one is puritanical enough to be wary of men wearing make-up in the street and alarmed at finding them making a noise in church. However, when the actors are separated from the audience by a solid proscenium arch and a series of conventions in acting and writing that dilute the entertainment into a mere social gathering then there may be some justification for reformation. Isn't this what Brecht had to do when he staged plays in the old Berlin theatre? He brought his chorus in front of the proscenium arch; shouted direct address at the audience; used every device he could to wake up the complacent public. A revolutionary theatre makes its assault as best it can. I am attracted by the possibilities of assaulting an audience, but I don't intend to take vigorous physical action until I find myself in a partisan group with something important to say. If we are to get into trouble with the police, I want it to be over an issue of real importance.

But let us get down to practical details, and leave theory in the background. There are a few simple points to be cleared up.

Is it more difficult to act in the round than on a conventional stage? No, not essentially, but most actors have been trained solely for the proscenium theatre, and have had most of their experience there; this may form a barrier to their achievements on a central stage. But young children play naturally in the round, and, unless they are pushed by those who know about stages on to a stage, their early dramatic play is usually completely in the round. This fascinating subject is thoroughly dealt with by Peter Slade in his book *Child Drama* in which he says, "At the risk of offending many well-disposed and genuine child lovers, it is, however, necessary to state that the proscenium form of theatre has disastrous effects on the genuine drama of the Child."★

Of course, much of the material we are now dealing with has no place in the creative drama of young children. For the most part they are unconcerned with an audience, and their acting area is unconfined other than within the limits of the room in use. It is as wrong, I think, to try and impose on young children even the formal acting of a theatre in the round as it is to put them on a proscenium stage. A good point lies behind Slade's emphasis that there is a difference between *acting* in the round and *performing* in the round.

Some professional actors quickly find their way to acting in the round, acting that has what we usually identify as absolute sincerity. When it is achieved it is so completely convincing as to defy analysis. Two young actors at the Victoria Theatre excelled in this quality. Heather Stoney joined the company, having had several years experience in conventional theatre work. But she had no difficulty in bringing on to the central stage the appearance of complete conviction that had already been a characteristic of her performances on the proscenium stage. She fulfilled the busy demands of a repertory theatre, playing many different parts with a brilliance that I found astonishing. Similarly, Bernard Gallagher, no matter what part he played, always brought to each performance a reality and polish that were deeply exciting. He could do this in such different roles as those already mentioned, the husband in de Hartog's *The Fourposter* and the Jew in Marlowe's *Jew of Malta*. In this last play he managed to give a completely acceptable vision of lifelike action while exploiting to the full the melodrama and richly farcical events that speed this play to its tragi-comic ending. Both these actors, then, performed with great sincerity, and it is a quality that is of the highest value in a theatre in the round; but there is probably more to it than this, though I am aware that the quality I am attempting to describe

★ Peter Slade, *Child Drama* (University of London Press Ltd.).

would probably be welcome on any stage, not just a central one; it is a question of subtle changes in emphasis. Calling to mind the performances of these two young actors, it seems to me that they achieved a special blend of what is often called "externalisation" and what is usually meant by "feeling". On the one hand an actor uses for material his observations of real life, as Garrick watched the poor madman who had accidentally killed his baby daughter and found here the inspiration for part of Lear's madness, or as Olivier observed the walk, gestures and speech rhythms of the Negro in preparation for his great performance as Othello. On the other hand there is the inner conviction derived from a study of the character one is about to play, the motivation, the emotional drives implied by the author, that must be felt if they are to be expressed. The former, if overdone, can degenerate into caricature; while the latter can put the actor himself to immense pains without giving any message at all to the audience, or, even worse, the actor may be so anxious not to overdo things that he will arrive at a state of maximum personal inertia. Neither of these extremes is acceptable; yet externalisation is as necessary as feeling, and it is the way an actor chooses between them, or arrives at a happy balance that identifies him as a good actor—at least for theatre in the round.

Young professional actors usually have little difficulty in discovering the techniques of acting on a central stage and though experienced actors may have greater misgivings they may soon become proficient and positively excited by the new challenge. As for amateurs, the same arguments arise; a long and limited experience of proscenium acting may be (but need not be) a hindrance, while inexperience and sense and enthusiasm will find the central stage as easy if not easier than the proscenium stage.

For some people certain conventions harden into axioms. Anyone, actor or member of an audience, who is convinced that you cannot act with your back, or that you must stand with your upstage foot forward, is unlikely to take kindly to a central stage. Such conventional notions may grow into a barrier between people in the audience and enjoyment of theatre in the round. Of course, conventions that have become so destructive are open to criticism. Here is an intriguing comment, made in 1888, on conventions of the proscenium stage:

> I can hardly have any illusions as to the possibility of getting the actor to play *to* the audience, instead of *with* it, however, desirable that might be. I do not dream of ever seeing the actor

turn his back completely throughout the whole of an important scene, but I do earnestly wish that crucial scenes should not be played as though they were duets intended to be applauded. I should like them to be given in the place indicated by the situation. No revolutions, then, but just a few small modifications; if we could have the stalls raised so that the spectator's eye could be above the level of the actor's knee and, most important of all, a *small* stage and a *small* house—and then perhaps a new dramatic art might arise, and at any rate the theatre might again become an institution for the enjoyment of cultured people.*

Strindberg here voices some of the stylistic principles of the realistic drama that can fairly be extended to the plays of Chekhov, Ibsen and to the majority of European writers of the first half of the twentieth century. There is no profit in wondering what Strindberg would have thought of theatre in the round; but it does answer his demands aptly enough, at least for certain points of acting technique and of staging.

What of diction and projection? Much has been said about the decline in vocal clarity among young actors. I believe this to be justified. Too many actors have poor diction; their breath control is poor, their articulation slipshod, and their range of tone very limited. As actors, they have only limited use on any stage (though they may do well enough, with the aid of microphones, on television or film).

So we come to the question of projection. If this means knocking them cold in the gallery (and spitting at the front rows of the stalls), obviously it has no place in our small theatre. On the other hand, an actor who estimates that he will need the same force to communicate with the five rows of theatre in the round as with five rows in a proscenium theatre may disappoint half his audience. But I don't think projection is simply a matter of loudness or force. Quietness and clarity can carry a long way. And I think that clarity of diction is of the utmost importance to an actor on a central stage. He must then find the characteristics of the theatre in relation to his voice (acoustics being what they are) and use the range of forces and of speeds that do not blur his clarity, choosing what is appropriate to play, character and event.

It follows from what has been said about the smallness of theatre in the round, about lighting and about the actors' use of movement, that stage make-up should not be excessive. Roughly speaking, what

* Strindberg, *Preface to Miss Julie.*

14. "Dragons Are Dangerous", performed at Wallis's Cayton Bay Holiday Camp.

15. The Playhouse Theatre, Houston, Texas.

16. "The Staffordshire Rebels" at the Victoria Theatre, Stoke-on-Trent. *(Photo Ian Stone.)*

17. The Arena Theatre, Washington, DC.

the actor sees in his mirror will be what the audience sees. A conventional stage make-up is inappropriate—except for the actor who is playing the part of an actor in stage make-up. Where possible it is best to use no make-up at all. When we presented *Easter* and *The Birthday Party* in repertoire, Dona Martyn played the parts of Eleonora and then of Meg. In neither case did she use make-up; but of course costume was very important, and hair-style completed the picture. For Eleonora, a school tunic, hair in plaits; for Meg a dirty overall, sloppy slippers, untidy hair hanging down.

However, the question of disguise (make-up being a part of disguise) includes the other aspects of characterisation, and it may be worth saying something about Dona Martyn's performances in these two parts. Let us put the picture into motion.

Eleonora is a girl of sixteen; she has a wonderful entrance into the play. Only the boy Benjamin is on stage, doing his homework at the table. In comes Eleonora, carrying a yellow daffodil in a pot. She puts the plant on the table, apparently not noticing Benjamin. She goes to the sideboard, gets a jug of water; waters the plant, returns the jug and then sits down opposite Benjamin. She watches him, copying his movements; as he becomes more and more aware of this, he slowly abandons his work and looks at her in astonishment—an astonishment reflected by her. Then she points at the daffodil and says: "Do you know what that is?" This is a moment of deep mystery; and to enjoy its depths we depend on absolute conviction from the actors, and a completely convincing picture of the characters (make-up and all).

In *The Birthday Party*, Meg is a slovenly, simply, seedy middle-aged landlady:

> *The living room of a house in a seaside town. A door leading to the hall down left. Back door and small window up left. Kitchen hatch, centre back. Kitchen door up right. Table and chairs, centre.*
>
> PETEY *enters from the door on the left with a paper and sits at the table. He begins to read.* MEG's *voice comes through the kitchen hatch.*
>
> MEG: Is that you, Petey?
>
> > *Pause.*
>
> Petey, is that you?
>
> > *Pause.*
>
> Petey?
>
> PETEY: What?

F

MEG: Is that you?

PETEY: Yes, it's me.

MEG: What? (*Her face appears at the hatch.*) Are you back?

PETEY: Yes.

MEG: I've got your cornflakes ready. (*She disappears, and reappears.*) Here's your cornflakes.

He rises and takes the plate from her, sits at the table, props up the paper, and begins to eat. MEG *enters by the kitchen door.* Are they nice?

PETEY: Very nice.

MEG: I thought they'd be nice. (*She sits at the table.*) You got your paper?

PETEY: Yes.

MEG: Is it good?

PETEY: Not bad.

MEG: What does it say?

PETEY: Nothing much.

MEG: You read me out some nice bits yesterday.

PETEY: Yes, well I haven't finished this one yet.

MEG: Will you tell me when you come to something good?

PETEY: Yes.

Pause.

MEG: Have you been working hard this morning?

PETEY: No. Just stacked a few of the old chairs. Cleaned up a bit.

MEG: Is it nice out?

PETEY: Very nice.

Pause.

MEG: Is Stanley up yet?

PETEY: I don't know. Is he?

MEG: I don't know. I haven't seen him down yet.

PETEY: Well then, he can't be up.

MEG: Haven't you seen him down?

PETEY: I've only just come in.

MEG: He must be still asleep.*

But the naked face is only one extreme. The other extreme can often be noticed when a good actor uses a mask. I recall a student at the Central School playing Agave in *The Bacchae*; her mask displayed quite clearly the joyous triumph of the opening sequences, and then it appeared to change, with the scene, to show doubt, then

* Harold Pinter, *The Birthday Party* (Methuen).

frenzy and then uttermost grief. It is moments like these that increase one's wonder at the theatre and admiration of the actor's skill, and set one pondering about the techniques of make-up! I have not seen masks extensively used in the round. It might be interesting to try a two faced figure—of the sort one finds among Indian marionettes. But we must never forget that make-up cannot be better than the actor's performance; it is never a substitute for good acting.

Sometimes a young actor is called on to play a small and mature part in a realistic play, and great acting cannot help since little acting is called for. A man may resort to moustaches, beards and grey hair. But there comes a point when greasepaint must be used. It should be applied much as a skilled representational portrait painter uses paint to turn a flat surface into a convincing three-dimensional likeness. Not easy. The implication is that the actor must also be a painter as skilled as Botticelli or Rubens or Annigoni. Certainly he should study the great painters. But at least he starts with a face, and, if he is not quite as good a painter as Rembrandt, he should do as little to it as possible.

10
Stage Management

THE usual organisation of backstage scarcely applies to theatre in the round. There need be only a very small staff—no stage-hands, fly-men, and no scene painters. Most of the work can probably be handled by a stage manager with one or two assistants. Let us look at some of their special jobs and unexpected tasks.

During rehearsals, when a movement is fixed, more or less, the stage manager must note it in the prompt copy. How is this done? In a realistic play, it is usually possible to make simple references to the features of the room and to the furniture, "x to door", "move behind armchair", and so on. On an empty stage, or in an abstract setting, there may be no such features. The stage manager may now like to make a simple grid of the stage—and note what are virtually map references. As a rule, though, it is sufficient to make centre-line co-ordinates and simply indicate the positions and moves in a series of quick diagrams. The stage manager will be helped if he always sits on the same side of the acting area, preferably related to his control position during performance.

A well rehearsed play does not need a prompter, and provided actors know from their first rehearsal that they will perform without one they seldom get into difficulties. A forgotten line can usually be dealt with by other actors. This is not just theory. Ever since our first season in Scarborough we have had no prompter, and only once has a really nasty moment occurred, and that was through laziness.

Amateur actors, who often have too little time to rehearse properly, may cling to the security of a prompter; he is best placed at the end of a front row. There is usually no need to supply him with a torch or special light, as light-spill from the acting area will be sufficient for him to follow the script comfortably.

The stage manager will usually have the job of looking after the wardrobe—a job he may delegate to a particular assistant. There are special points to watch. With costume, as with make-up, the audience will see what the actor sees in his mirror. Period costume in a realistic production should be made to stand close examination—and zip fasteners will usually show down the back of a dress. After a performance of *Wuthering Heights* a member of the audience commented that Heathcliff would not have worn Phillip's rubber soles.

On a stage that has so little scenic colour, costumes provide an important element in décor, and should be considered with great care. A good hire firm will usually meet the challenge willingly. For a production of *Victoria Regina*, Simmons provided us with several authentic Victorian costumes and some specially made for our performance. It is very important to make sure that costumes are made properly, fit properly and that they are clean. Make-up is often difficult to get off theatrical costumes, and for ordinary theatre purposes it does not matter; but it will probably spoil a costume in the round. There is a lot to be said in favour of home-made costumes, provided they are well made. The least trailing bit of thread will show, and a split seam at your back cannot be concealed merely by facing the audience. These are obvious comments, and superficial; of course, a play may require dirty, ill-fitting costumes with dangling threads galore, split seams and rag patches. In such a play as *The Lower Depths* it may be very important to have rags and tatters that are truly convincing.

There is no need for a scenic artist in a theatre in the round. But the setting must be carefully planned, the furniture, costumes and props carefully chosen. The producer may take responsibility for all of these himself, or he may rely on a designer (particularly for costumes if they are to be made for the production), but in a fairly simple production the supervision of all these things will fall to the stage manager.

A realistic play usually requires great attention to the details of furniture and dressing the stage. The furniture may be and generally should be arranged with direct reference to reality. There is no need to put that settee (where it is so often put on the proscenium stage) with one end towards the fireplace so that the actors sitting on it face, not the fire, but the audience. The fourth wall is there, to be used. It is important to know how people arrange their rooms and how a room is related architecturally to a house. Be sure that furniture can stand being looked at from all round.

On the subject of furniture, a limitation of theatre in the round arises out of the inadvisability of using tall pieces such as grandfather clocks, tallboys, kitchen dressers and suchlike that will obscure sightlines. If absolutely necessary to a play such items can be set by a gangway. Hung pictures and mirrors may also pose problems; where they cannot equally well be placed to stand on a table, a completely empty frame can be suspended—though this may not be appropriate to a severely realistic production.

For a play such as *A Likely Tale* by Gerald Savory, the realistic and sentimental story will be greatly helped by a stage that is fully furnished, paying attention to every sort of detail from the cake stand to the collection of china, from the chairs and table to the sandwiches that provide such a delightfully comic scene. By contrast, it is possible to present *The Ark* by James Saunders, as we did, with only a single block, a cube of 18 in., on stage. This was moved from one end of the acting area to the other when a change of scene was necessary; nothing else.

A production of *A Sense of Loss* by J. W. James made use of two such blocks, set on a floor covered with a specially designed pattern of tiles in blue and white. There were many scenes in this play, starting at a bus stop, going into a dance hall, a bedroom, an office and other places. The actors moved these blocks informally at the break of each scene. An audience looks down on to the acting area of a theatre in the round so that the floor covering becomes important. Sometimes it is sensible to use a specially painted floorcloth, sometimes carpets, rugs, lino or some special surface—sand, perhaps, or different levels of timber.

A multi-room set can be defined not only by the lay-out of the furniture but also by the different floor-coverings, and, where possible, by the different light-fittings hanging from overhead. A play that requires this kind of setting is *Five Finger Exercise* by Peter Shaffer; the walls of the rooms need no other material than the appropriate performances of the actors—and the imaginations of the audience.

For David Campton's *Frankenstein* the stage was divided into two areas. One remained the laboratory of Frankenstein, the place where the monster would be brought to life; the other area, with a little moving of chairs, became either Frankenstein's drawing room, or the study as required. The stage was also divided for *Wuthering Heights* by Jurneman Winch, one half representing the moors (a number of different levels covered roughly with flooring felt) and the other representing each of the interior scenes.

Sometimes difficult scenic effects must be achieved by lighting. In Scarborough we have presented two plays at the end of which the house is supposed to catch fire. In neither case did we achieve the effect successfully; particularly since it is obviously not advisable to use smoke—and where there's no smoke . . . The more successful of the two occasions was at the end of *The Pelican* by Strindberg; two characters are on stage, wrapping each other in a tight embrace as the light goes out. They comment on the smell of burning, on the noises (which were provided) and finally they collapse—in a pool of fluctuating orange light. The actors were good, but the fire was never very much more than an image in their minds. The other play, David Campton's *Roses Round the Door*, presented us with the added problem of many characters on stage, a good deal of action, and a supposedly hilarious situation; too difficult to bring off, at least in the Library Theatre at Scarborough.

Scene changes can be carried out in a number of ways. In some plays the actors may move the props and furniture. This may be appropriate in a play where there is a maidservant. A production of Laurence Housman's *Victoria Regina* made use of the same furniture throughout, a few pieces taken away or added from time to time, and the actual lay-out altered to suit each scene; the changes were done by two liveried flunkeys who also took part in the play. Sometimes it is possible to make swift changes in the dark between scenes, but I am not fond of this as the audience usually gets restless in the dark and tries to discover what is going on; better, probably, to bring up a little light specially for the scene change. If a complete change of furniture is required, taking up a few minutes, there is no reason why the stage managers should not work in full light—the audience will probably enjoy watching, particularly if the change is well organised and smoothly carried out. I don't think an audience is worried by seeing "the works" in this way, particularly if the change is clearly defined by the lowering of lights to blackout at the end of the scene, then lights come up for the change, go again to darkness at the conclusion of the change, and then come up again for the play to resume.

The stage manager usually has to prepare any sound effects called for in a play. It has already been suggested that a loudspeaker should be housed centrally above the acting area. In realistic plays most "off-stage" sound effects should come through this speaker. Otherwise noise from outside the acting area will tend to take the attention of at least part of the audience away from the stage into the auditorium. Surely the intention with most such effects is to indicate what the characters on stage hear? Some people suppose that stereophonic effects can easily be used in the round. This is not so. A series of loudspeakers round the theate will have no useful effect whatever. They will simply draw the audience's attention away from the acting area to the back of the seating where the nearest loudspeaker will, of course, be clearly heard. A limited use of stereophony can be obtained by having separate loudspeakers on the acting area, and switching from one to the other, but this is not dependent on stereophonic recordings or amplification and is a trick not much required. As with so many technical devices in the theatre, sound systems should serve the actor and not draw attention to their own cleverness. A brilliant technician may like to demonstrate his skill, and he should be given an opportunity to do so. But such a demonstration will rarely fit in with the production of a play. It follows that a special problem for theatre in the round is the provision of voices off, and conversations where one character is on stage and another supposedly in the next room. I would prefer either to have both characters on stage (with a split set, perhaps, presenting both rooms), or to have the off-stage voice coming over the central loudspeaker, or to cut the sequence. But if none of these solutions is fair to the play, then voices off there must be.

A common stage effect that can be particularly useful in theatre in the round, and which has been very successful in several Scarborough productions, is to wire up a telephone so that the off-stage voice can be clearly heard. It is simple to feed into the telephone the signal from a tape-recorder, and to provide the voice in this way.

I do not like, in any theatre, the use of real candles, flaming torches, or actual oil-lamps. There are always people (I am one) who are scared that something may catch fire, and there is no sense in frightening them—and taking the very real risk that always surrounds naked flame. Even matches can be dangerous, though most actors are very adept at using them properly. My policy, and advice, is to avoid them all if possible. A very effective oil lamp in Strindbergs' *The Pariah* was wired electrically and controlled by dimmer; it deceived most people.

Having emphasised reality, I find that I am now advocating tricks. The point is that such tricks must be judged by very severe standards if they are to succeed in the round.

Properties must be chosen with the same care that is called for by costumes and furniture. Things will look very much what they are, and it is usually better to get the real thing rather than to try and fake it. Trouble may arise with food. It is usually difficult to eat and drink on stage the meals that playwrights refer to. In a comedy by Catherine Prynne called *The Ornamental Hermit*, a situation of mistaken identity meant that an actor had to eat two breakfasts, one after the other; fortunately the young actor playing this part had a remarkable appetite and enjoyed the opportunity. So did the audience—real fried eggs smell so nice! On most stages it is possible to pour out only half cups of tea (and the playwright hardly gives the actors time to drink this, as a rule), but an audience looking down on to the stage will detect such behaviour—and will be disappointed. It may be better to cut the second cup and make a proper job of the first. At the beginning of *Five Finger Exercise* there is a breakfast. David Jarrett, who played Clive, joined us in Scarborough, having just played the part elsewhere. He was surprised to find that he couldn't get away with a little scrambled egg on a large plate, and that what he left of toast and marmalade would be clearly seen by all the audience; he settled for a simpler breakfast on a more or less realistic scale. And then, incidentally, worked hard on what became an outstanding performance.

The reality of food can be too interesting to an audience. Aubrey Colin's play *Father Matthew* tells an interesting story of intolerance within the circle of a family; at the height of strong feelings, when the family is most divided, some not speaking to others, lunchtime comes. Father Matthew asks his family to gather round the table, which they do more or less unwillingly; then a family conversation begins and suddenly provokes everyone into cheerfulness and acceptance. It is not a glib ending. We are not to suppose that understanding suddenly descends, but that everyone recognises the necessity of eating together if not of thinking alike. An open conclusion. On our stage the ending was spoiled because the audience seemed more interested in the fact that there was a real joint, real cider, real lettuce, real tomatoes. . . . After the play, as the audience left the theatre, many of them went to the table to rejoice in the reality of these things. I doubt if many of them got the reality of the play.

In Denis Cannan's *Captain Carvallo* a pie is made at the beginning of the first scene. In the Scarborough production this was later taken out of the oven, apparently baked to a nice brown; and an audible noise of astonishment went up from the audience. A simple trick, having the cooked pie already set in the oven, this did not cause any break in the action nor weaken any important moment in the play.

Tricks may also have to be played in such a scene as the dinner
G

party in Noel Coward's *Fallen Angels*. Here the point is very much that a full dinner is eaten, but the actresses simply cannot cope with real food in such quantities. Special dishes have to be made that look substantial but are not. Our catering manager devised mushrooms in aspic (we christened them "Fallen Angels") to do for oysters; steaks had to be bread in gravy—a familiar standby; and extra light-weight eclairs were made for sweet. Champagne is a standard property. . . .

11
Choice of Play

So much concern with the theatre turns on the written play that a possible criticism of theatre in the round is that it limits our choice. In fact this is not really true, except as far as it is true of any form of theatre. I suppose there is no form of theatre that can stage every sort of play. But no theatre will ever have to do so; there are far too many plays, and only a selection can be made for presentation. A sensible director or dramaturge will not, of course, choose plays that are only suitable for other and more appropriate theatres. It is not necessary, then, to judge theatre in the round on what it cannot do if what it can do is as good and plentiful as in fact it is.

All the same, we may learn more about theatre in the round if we examine its reputed limitations in choice of play. Obviously a play that depends considerably on scenic effect may present real difficulties. For instance, I should hesitate before presenting Flecker's *Hassan* with its scene where the basket is hoisted aloft carrying, one by one, the important night wanderers to their mysterious destination. But come to think of it, such a scene could easily be staged in a well-equipped theatre in the round that had good overhead catwalks and roof void. If it could not easily be done in Scarborough, for instance, this is because the Library Theatre is not properly equipped, and presents the same sort of limitations that you may find in any temporary fit-up theatre. Besides, such limitations could, if absolutely necessary, be overcome. The play is not a likely choice for Scarborough because of the size of its cast, but if it were chosen it would be because of the whole exciting story, the splendour of the dialogue, the interesting and exotic characters, the humour, the excitement. What I am getting at is that this play, like most worthwhile plays, is about events and about people and not about scenery. Scenic effects are seldom crucial. Where they are crucial, they may be contrived. Most productions of *Hassan* are cut and much edited for various reasons. In Scarborough the basket would be lowered from a peripheral stage, of the sort already mentioned for use in *Cock and Bull Story*.

In *Captain Carvallo* there is much ado about hiding in a cupboard under the stairs; for theatre in the round the cupboard was turned into a large wooden chest which served perfectly well, and in no way spoiled the dramatist's fun.

Plays that certainly used to rely on scenic spectacle were the old melodramas and pantomimes. They have gone out of fashion now, and their attraction has been taken over by the spectacular film. I am very fond of many of these old plays, but must admit that they could not easily be presented in the round without considerable modification to the author's original intention. All the same there are many melodramas which might be worth reviving if only because they are not seen any more on the picture-frame stage (where they would be costly to mount). In particular, such plays as, for example, *Black-Eyed Susan*, *The Ticket of Leave Man*, *The Dumb Man of Manchester*, and the Irish plays of Boucicault, all have considerable appeal. Melodramas were continually written, adapted and pirated in their heyday, and it would be no sacrilege to adapt them for a special form of stage now. Plays such as *The Beggar's Opera*, other ballad operas and, indeed, grand opera might be considered too difficult; but, though they require special techniques, they can without much trouble be staged in theatre in the round and have been frequently so performed in the United States.

Of all my favourite plays the ones that I hesitate most to present in the round are Restoration comedies. An essential quality of such plays as *The Provok'd Husband* or *The Country Wife* or *The Man of Mode* is that each play holds up (as 'twere) a mirror to its original audience. The mirror image is best suggested in a small theatre with a modest picture-frame stage which marks the mirror surface, and with, essentially, a fore-stage that has architecturally integrated side doors. The fore-stage provides a sort of no-man's-land between mirror and spectator from which asides and comments on behalf of the audience can be made by the actors (usually conventional moral judgements). The doors are important to provide notional rooms— "Lock the door, Madam", says Horner to Lady Fidget, and in a moment he goes out at another door for off-stage action in her company; they are sought almost immediately by Mrs Squeamish who goes off by yet another door. The four proscenium doors make the action plain; theatre in the round might dilute the comedy. Might.

But, in spite of my caution, which is only theoretical, why not try and see?

The Studio Theatre Company had great fun with Marivaux's *The Game of Love and Chance*. Its conventions are not exactly those of our Restoration comedies, but there is enough in common to suppose that where one succeeds the other might also.

In restoration comedy many lines need to be spoken directly to the audience, so do soliloquys in Elizabethan plays; and much of the dialogue in nineteenth-century melodrama seems designed to be shouted to the back of the gallery. Each written for a different sort of theatre. Modern productions of these kinds of play will deal with such problems in very different ways. They are problems, and they are capable of solution in theatre in the round as in any other form of theatre.

In the end I find it difficult to admit that any play I would really like to do would suffer from production in the round. I have listened to theories suggesting that, for example, plays that have a claustrophobic atmosphere cannot be presented satisfactorily, and I must admit the theory can be elaborated very convincingly, until you look at the plays in question, which include Pinter's *Birthday Party*, Sartre's *Huis Clos*, Strindberg's *Miss Julie*, all of which have been presented in the round and have been exceptionally successful. I am still waiting to be convinced of some important limitation that is inherent in theatre in the round and is not just a notion in the mind of a deft theoretician.

On the other hand, one has real favourites. Let me start off with an author who seems to me to benefit greatly from the central stage. Strindberg. And firstly, his play *Miss Julie*. I have already quoted the author's preface to the play. It seems as though he writes in a style that suggests a self-contained pocket of reality, a small reality of intense power. If the actors play to each other (and not to the audience), if they move and speak with concentration on the relationship between them and with no apparent regard for the audience, then this small vision of reality has an absorbing and tremendous appeal. This seems to be what the playwright wanted. Other plays by Strindberg have also worked well in our theatre, including *Easter*, *Lucky Peter's Travels*, *The Pariah*, *The Pelican* and *Playing with Fire*: we have not yet done *The Father* simply because, so far, we have not had the actor for the part. But I hope to remedy this soon, and to continue mining this playwright's vein of riches.

I like sentimentality in the theatre, particularly when it is combined with a more or less epic treatment. A good example of this kind of play is *Peer Gynt*, which I have yet to see in the round; but we have presented a number of plays, mostly biographical, that have provided the pleasures of this genre. The first of them was Jurneman Winch's *Turn Right at the Crossroads*; another favourite was *A Sense of Loss*; and it was great fun to do *The Play of Mata Hari* by Michael Stott. Joan Macalpine made an adaptation of *David Copperfield* in this style, and Alan Stockwell gave us a challenging and highly original script called *The Bed Life of a Mad Boy*. Strindberg's *Lucky Peter's Travels* demanded a fairly complicated setting, made out of painter's ladders and builder's boards, but gave us the opportunities we wanted for a simple, sweeping performance. Each of these plays is broken into short scenes, requires the simplest of staging, explores fully the character of one person and provides the rest of the actors with several parts apiece. In these plays it is not just the sentimentality that appeals to me; it is also the attempt to compress into the short time of a single performance the whole of a man's life, or as much of it as gives the impression of a whole existence.

I recall a brilliant amateur performance of *The Bald Prima Donna* by the Hull Garrett Players, who have done many excellent theatre in the round productions. Here the actors moved in the formal patterns of a dance, precisely timed, and spoke as isolated characters to each other and to the audience without change of style. And the maid-servant springs marvellously to life in a soliloquy addressed to a surrounding audience. This is precisely what Ionesco seems to demand in the play. I enjoyed the production (and saw it twice for no other reason) but must confess that I would never attempt anything of the sort myself; my talent does not lie in careful choreographic organisation.

There are always people who want to know how Shakespeare works in the round. Answer—very well. Certain of his plays, such as *Twelfth Night* and *As You Like It* seem to have been written for a sort of central staging and they present no difficulties at all. Other plays, for instance *The Tempest* and *Romeo and Juliet*, may demand a playhouse of another particular type. I look forward to the day when it is possible to see them done on a stage that is appropriate. Meanwhile it is not much sillier to do them in the round than it is to shove them on a picture-frame stage. In Margo Jones' production of *Romeo and Juliet* the separation of the lovers in the balcony scene was achieved by Romeo standing, as in the garden, on one side of the stage, and Juliet standing on the other side, as on a balcony, each isolated in separate canopies of light; there is nothing unconvincing about this provided the actors can act and the audience can understand the words.

In my production of *Hamlet*, using a script carefully edited by Professor Empson, the play was presented without any interval. Very little was cut; all the characters remained; no attempt was made to eradicate political comment or subject; cutting was virtually confined to repetitions (many of them, of course, textual accretions) and to obscurities. Each scene flowed immediately into the next, without pause, without scene change and without uncalled-for musical or other flourish. The actors spoke lightly and swiftly but with as much change of pace and intensity as the lines seemed to demand. All this was no more than an attempt at honest workmanship. A number of problems had to be dealt with. Firstly, the ghost in the cellarage. The actor is clearly meant to be under the stage. And what is more, the audience is expected to hear him there. We performed on a solid, untrapped floor. The actor, Richard Gill, evolved the solution to the problem in this sequence. He merely crossed the stage, apparently unseen by the other characters, speaking as he moved. In the comparatively dark scene, and with a black velvet cloak over his armour he indeed appeared ghostly and convincing, even if not quite in the manner intended. We may not have observed the word, but we got the spirit, as it were.

Finally, the grave. Again this clearly requires a trapped area. For this production a rectangular wooden framework, about eight inches high and covered with pieces of underfelt, was constructed to represent the grave; it was carried on to the stage by the gravediggers and put down without ceremony. Then the first gravedigger laid his spade across the framework and seemed to lower himself down (he knelt within "the grave"); this was done with a skill that gave the audience great amusement, absolutely compatible with the scene.

Strictly speaking neither the problem of the grave, nor of the ghost in the cellarage, specifically belongs to theatre in the round. All that is wanted is a trap and any well equipped theatre, in the round or otherwise, should have traps. In this production no such facility was available. There are other difficult moments in *Hamlet* that depend on staging: one that I have never seen satisfactorily solved is the awkward poisoning of the Queen. "The poisoned cup," exclaims the King and does nothing to stop her drinking it. In my opinion this line will only make sense if the scene is staged (as was probably envisaged by the playwright) with the main action of the play performed on a platform, of the sort commonly assumed to have been erected for the Elizabethan public playhouse, and the duel between Laertes and Hamlet taking place in the middle of the theatre, on the floor of the arena; the Queen comes down from the platform to mop Hamlet's brow and she is there beside him when she takes the cup. The King sees her, but he is remote, on the high stage. Later, when Hamlet is dead, Fortinbras says, "Bear Hamlet's body to the stage", and he means just that. There are other moments in the play where both arena and platform are used, but this one is crucial. In other plays, too, notably *Romeo and Juliet* and *Antony and Cleopatra*, a similar staging technique might answer satisfactorily many problems that have usually been poorly solved. But this is not the place to go into such details.

There is much to be said in favour of plays written especially for theatre in the round. Not only has the Studio Theatre Company, since its inception, included a high proportion of new plays in its repertoire, but we have deliberately set out to have the playwright as a working member of the company. For nearly ten years we had at least one resident dramatist, and for some months had five playwrights whose work was staged by the company, itself no more than ten people in all. These playwrights have, of course, done more than write. Usually they have also been actors. Although not many companies now deal with playwrights in this way, the precedent and fine example is there in the careers of Shakespeare, or Molière, or of Sophocles.

New plays written especially for theatre in the round, will, one hopes, assimilate some of the special qualities of this form of theatre, even if one is not quite sure what these qualities are. I ought to try and describe them. And I could start off with some personal prejudices, such as: the play should be written in one long sweep (don't divide it into two or three acts), it should be funny if possible, give me a good story (or plot) rich in events and let the characters follow accordingly (rather than a play primarily rich in characterisation), have as many changes of scene as you like, come and look at our audience and write a play that will rivet their attention. But this is vague and general stuff, and I haven't really begun to consider the form of theatre.

In our day and age the play is the beginning of each theatrical venture, and to start off with something new rather than something secondhand is obviously more exciting. Now many managers and directors want to find good new plays, and are prepared to present them when they find them; this seems to me to be needle in the haystack philosophy, for good new plays are just about this rare. I like to find a new play of promise merely, in the hope that the playwright will develop and write good plays eventually. Playwriting is a difficult job, and it is wrong to expect a first play to be good; if it is, the playwright will probably be a one-off merchant who will never write a better. It may seem a bit heartless to present an audience with a new play that I know is not good, is no more than promising merely. It would be so if most of the secondhand plays that have already been done in London were better. They are not. Most of the plays that are staged in London's West End are poor stuff, and many of the new plays that I put on are nothing like so poor. This is, of course, one man's judgement. But who else's judgement has one got? A critic who had given a series of very harsh reviews to our new plays was asked if he really thought they were all that bad; and he replied that they couldn't be any good as they hadn't been done in London; I asked how many plays he had seen in London, and he replied: none. So I'll trust my judgement.

It is not just the director who is excited about a new play. Certainly the author is; and he may even get so excited as to be a nuisance at rehearsals; as is usually expected of him. But I have seldom found him so. His excitement helps the actors, who usually enjoy creating roles that are quite new.

Some idea of the range of plays that can be done in theatre in the round can be grasped by looking at lists of plays done in a few such theatres. The range is wide. I have collected play-titles from Jack Mitcheley, from the BDL, as well as from the Pembroke Theatre, the Library Theatre in Scarborough and the Victoria Theatre; and from a few theatres in the round in the United States: at Tufts University, the Alley Theatre in Houston, the Arena Stage in Washington, DC. Over 800 plays, all done within the last twenty years, and covering new plays and old plays, classical plays and modern plays, comedies and tragedies, realistic plays and fantasies, sophisticated plays and children's plays, straight and musical plays. It would be difficult to think of a kind of play that is not represented. The facts suggest that there is very little limitation imposed by the central stage on choice of play; our choice is restricted by many considerations, of budget, of casting, of audience taste, of occasion, but it need scarcely be hindered by the demands of theatre in the round.

12
Economics

EVEN those people who have been most unattracted to theatre in the round, unconvinced by performances or by theoretical argument, usually concede that at least one thing to be said in its favour is that it is cheap. The word *cheap* can carry a pejorative flavour, but it needn't do so. There is much to welcome in a theatre that does not demand great expenditure. The continual emphasis that I have placed on the simplicity of theatre in the round is a pointer both to its excitement and its cheapness. But it is difficult to make convincing comparisons between the costs of running or building different forms of theatre, and the results would probably not mean very much anyhow, since money can be wasted and extravagance introduced into any budget, large or small. Equally, effective use of resources depends not so much on form of theatre as on the person who looks after the administration of the company.

However, roughly speaking, and all other things being equal as it were, an important economy certainly available when running a theatre in the round is the small demands it makes on scenery. The virtual absence of scenery means not only that little has to be spent on actual materials but also the technical staff can be fairly small. Further, paintshop and storage space may be modest. Fly tower and wingspaces are virtually unnecessary.

The small budget required for running a theatre in the round makes sense of our demand that the theatre shall have a small capacity. A sensible balance between expenditure and income from ticket sales can easily be maintained.

Clearly these points affect the design of a new building. A commercially viable theatre can be planned on a modest scale, involving small capital sums. If the point of reference in pricing a theatre is taken as the cost per seat, a theatre in the round is likely to cost less than half the price of a conventional theatre. But if the comparison is made on the basis of scale, then, since a theatre in the round can afford to run on a smaller scale, it may cost, in any given situation, as little as a fifth of the amount required for a proscenium theatre. For example, when the civic theatre at Newcastle-under-Lyme was being discussed, the first scheme considered was a conventional theatre. Careful calculation resulted in the recommended capacity being about 600, and the total cost about £250,000. A few years later, a second scheme envisaged a theatre in the round seating about 400 and costing £60,000. Since the plans were prepared by different architects and at different times these figures do not give an absolute comparison, but they indicate quite fairly the principle involved in costing.

So much for capital outlay. To return to revenue, there is a further issue. In these days when few professional theatres can function at all without subsidy, it is worth considering if a theatre in the round can make effective use of its subsidy.

First, does subsidy carry with it any precise obligations? The answer is no. Most people who are concerned with financing the arts simply accept that theatre is vaguely a good thing, and that if it cannot exist without help, then help must be given. However, there are some theatres that flourish without subsidy and many people feel that there must be at least a half-hearted bias in subsidised theatres towards a special policy. It may often be difficult to find the special-ness, but sometimes it is clear enough. In provincial repertory theatres subsidy accompanies a bias towards adequate rehearsal time, the replacing of weekly changes of programme by fortnightly, three, or four weekly changes; towards establishing a repertoire of plays instead of running each play for a solid week or so; towards the pre-sentation of new plays, of the classics and of the classics not often performed. The embodiment of details like these in a policy obviously depends more on the directors' resolutions than on the form of theatre.

But the directors will obviously be influenced by practical con-siderations. And in practice the Victoria Theatre at Stoke has set a fair example. Compared with other theatres of similar size or with a similar budget, or, importantly, with similar grants, its policy does seem to reflect more brightly than most the suggested implications of subsidy. Its plays are done in repertoire, there is considerable emphasis on new plays of quality and on classics, and rehearsals usually last for three or four weeks. There are various other less usual accents at Stoke including an attempt to establish a children's theatre where the needs of children are really understood, exploration of the possibilities of theatre in the round as a home for modern dance, and such activities as regular sessions of poetry and jazz. Most of these manifestations of policy are taken for granted by commentators who would make a point of welcoming them in a conventional theatre, simple because it is really obvious and natural for a small theatre in the round to take the lead in this way. It can so aptly afford to do so.

It is important to establish the fact that from an economic point of view theatre in the round is thoroughly sensible and that a theatre could be built and run for a company of professional actors to compare favourably with other forms of theatre. However, the theatrical profession (like most others) is very conservative and does not take kindly to what are supposed to be novel ideas; this is particularly so when the building of new theatres is anyhow a very rare thing, and, in a business as risky as the theatre is at best, the risk of building a theatre of this form is not likely to appeal to any person investing large sums of money.

Besides, building any sort of theatre is so expensive that private people are not likely to be attracted to it (unless they already have a quite specific idea of what they want to do: and this idea is likely to include the form of theatre). Our appetite for drama, then, must be satisfied some other way, and there has been an increasing demand, in this country, for civic theatres, built by municipal authorities. After the war the first full-sized theatre was built, after an interval of twenty years, by the city of Coventry. Then followed theatres at Croydon, Eastbourne, Bromley, Guildford, Leicester and many other towns and cities. Above all, the theatre at Nottingham, which, most people would agree, is the finest theatre in England.

Now these theatres are very different from each other as far as the number of seats is concerned; they have different facilities for the audience and backstage; their plan areas vary considerably and so do their costs. Further, apart from the buildings, the companies that occupy these theatres do so on terms that are as individual as you could hope for. If we were also to take into consideration companies that occupy existing buildings that have been taken over by municipal authorities, as at Sunderland, Hull, Crewe, Manchester and Rotherham, the complexity of civic theatre organisation is increased.

Most, though not all, of these civic theatres are fairly big buildings. Many of them have similar stage facilities, and the question of mutual aid naturally arises. There is much to be said in favour of the idea that there should be, throughout England, a number of civic theatres forming a circuit to share certain productions and touring companies from the metropolitan centres of drama, the National Theatre, the opera and ballet companies, as well as important foreign companies from, perhaps, the Moscow Arts Theatre, the Berliner Ensemble, or the New York Metropolitan Opera. Theatres in this circuit could also initiate and tour their own productions of plays, pantomimes, variety, music hall and so on. But (although I have only sketched what might in fact be a very magnificent and exciting scheme) the vision seems to have strictly limited application. The number of theatres in such a circuit must be small, say a dozen or so; and will naturally be limited, because of the size of theatres involved, to our major cities. This is perfectly sensible. But what about smaller cities and towns? Are they to be left without theatres, and persuaded, perhaps, to provide special transport for the people who want to enjoy entertainment in the big cities? The prospect is not attractive. Further, the circuit of civic theatres must necessarily imply a degree of standardisation and, however acceptable this may be as a price paid for getting the big theatre companies into the provinces, it clearly takes a lot of enjoyment out of what should be an exciting creative occupation, in which standardisation soon becomes a positive hindrance.

So there is every reason to advocate, as well as the big civic theatres, as much individual building as possible. I believe that every town with a population of, say, 50,000 or more could and should have its own professional theatre. I hope that such a theatre would be mainly concerned with the staging of plays and similar entertainments; it would be a building quite unique, even deliberately as unlike as any other theatre as possible, and the company of actors working in it would belong to the community, staging plays for this particular audience, and new plays as often as possible. The actors and the audience should share tastes, experiences, problems, attitudes to life. The stage should really mirror the community; it is true that life's great problems are universal, but the drama is also concerned with details, and details vary richly from locality to locality. So should the theatre. Paradoxically, I guess, any theatre that pursues such an individualistic policy is likely to become famous; a theatre of conventional pattern is not worth much trouble to visit, since familiar plays may be seen anywhere, but a company presenting highly original work in a unique theatre cannot be enjoyed except by going to see it.

This argument can be extended a bit to mollify those who might be tempted to copy someone else's civic theatre but find, for one reason or another, that it is not practical. For the National Theatre can always be seen in London. The Nottingham Playhouse remains in Nottingham. Both are worth going to see, and people know this and go to see them. This points favourably towards the idea of providing as far as possible for the creative aspects of theatre as opposed to standard concepts, and noting that the size of the community does not impose a limitation here, but rather, I suggest, the smaller the community the greater the opportunity for escaping standardisation and enjoying individuality. Of course the advantages of having a small creative theatre are usually recognised by even the strongest advocate of the big civic theatre, and there is every reason to propose that even a large theatre is not enough but should be accompanied by a small theatre.

A small theatre in the round, such as our Theatre Two, serving the community with a fairly original programme of plays, would probably be used to work in repertoire. The advantages of the repertoire system are well known, but it is worth going over them. Experience in most of our provincial repertory theatres (which do not employ this system) shows that it is difficult to maintain high standards of performance and that a particular play that may not be popular has a depressing effect in the theatre where slender audiences for several weeks not only discourage the actors but break the rhythm of attendance. A new play, as so often happens in these theatres, usually has not time to earn its reputation in the town and is therefore seldom risked. But if plays are presented in repertoire the actors have a more varied and rewarding work schedule that tends to lead to higher standards of performance. A successful play can easily be held in the repertoire for extra time, and an unconventional play can be nursed along until it establishes itself. This is only half the argument; of course the system requires very careful organisation (which means extra staff and offices) and may cost more in salaries of actors and in publicity. Wherever it has been tried, at the Belgrade, at Nottingham Playhouse, at Dundee, the advantages are generally agreed to outweigh the snags. Now each of these theatres has a very substantial difficulty to overcome that does not apply to theatre in the round—as has been discovered at the Victoria Theatre. This is the cost of scenery and its manipulation and storage. A picture-frame stage virtually necessitates scenery, and some plays have several settings. Each play in the repertoire presents extra demands not only in the basic scenic materials, but also in the labour of shifting the scenery and storing it. Even in a well equipped theatre, such as the Nottingham Playhouse, the extra expense is a real burden. The usual answer might be merely to demand a bigger auditorium so that the expenses can be met. But this does not help us if we are deliberately trying to build a small theatre. Here is where theatre in the round offers a particularly happy solution; the stage does not require scenery—indeed, as has been indicated already, it is probably at its best when the stage is empty of all but actors. The summer theatre in the round at Scarborough has been able to hold seven plays in repertoire (about as many as any small company of actors would be willing to keep going), and play each at successive performances, without any scenic store, and without any extra stage management personnel, or indeed any extra working hours for the usual small staff. If the repertoire system is important, this is an important advantage that theatre in the round offers; I put it no more strongly than that because, strange to say, I am not yet personally convinced that the repertoire system is always better than the more usual short run schedule (particularly when one sees the success of this method at such a theatre as the Library Theatre in Manchester).

So far we have been looking at the full-time professional theatre. Many civic authorities would prefer a theatre that could provide for visiting companies and for local amateur groups. Indeed, in some quarters the idea of a civic theatre is that it should provide entirely for amateurs. Theatre in the round is still worth considering. It should by now have been established that this form of theatre is perfectly valid for amateurs and that its restrictions are no more serious than those of any other particular form of theatre. The combined activities of the professional and amateur groups in Scarborough provide us with examples of a touring company of professional actors using the same theatre as the various amateur groups in the town, as well as the festivals organised by the area branch of the BDL and to which come amateur societies from all over the country.

As far as building costs are concerned, it is important to consider that a small civic theatre in the round might be a very inexpensive building indeed. The cost of the proposed theatre at Newcastle-under-Lyme included all the facilities that might be expected to go with a theatre. But Theatre Two could easily grow out of a converted building. Warehouses, chapels, schoolrooms and so on often present good opportunities for conversion, and depending on the existing facilities such a conversion might easily be carried out for two or three thousand pounds. The Victoria Theatre, converted from a cinema, should have cost about ten thousand pounds; we didn't have the money and completed the initial conversion for five thousand, though further necessary improvements will probably demand the balance. The Scarborough theatre in the round is a temporary conversion; either of two rooms is used, and all stage lighting, portable rostrums for raising the seating and other equipment is brought in for the setting up of the theatre. Total cost of the equipment is about two thousand pounds.

But cheap though these examples may be, a word of warning is necessary. Many magnificent theatres have been spoiled by false economies. Even the Belgrade Theatre, so obviously trying to do things properly in the foyer, is severely handicapped backstage. Stories are told of theatres built without dressing rooms (by mistake), or without adequate provision for stage lighting. And if it is possible to build an expensive theatre on the cheap, it is certainly possible to build an inexpensive theatre on the cheap too. Both can be spoiled. The actual cost of building a theatre does not determine whether it is well or badly designed, nor if it is adequately or distressingly equipped. The fact that a small theatre in the round can be built, or converted from an existing building, very cheaply, does not absolve us from the necessity of doing the job properly, and the cost will vary depending on the starting point and the expectations we have of the theatre.

Many municipal authorities want to have a theatre that will be able to take the National Theatre company when it comes on tour, house a resident repertory company, provide for the needs of the local amateur groups, convert into a dance hall, boxing ring, wrestling arena, bingo palace, banqueting hall, cinema, concert room; it should not cost more than £60,000 to build. The demand is an impossible one, of course, and most experienced theatre people say immediately that a multi-purpose theatre is only feasible either on a very small scale indeed or else with the expenditure of vast sums of money on elaborate machinery. They would probably then suggest, as I have just done, that if a theatre is to be built, it must be done properly; they would go on, as I would not, to say that every stage must have a grid tower of at least two and a half times the height of the proscenium opening; wing space must add up to at least the width of the acting area again; and so on. The cost will probably be at least a quarter of a million pounds which is once again more than the local authority is prepared to spend. All this because of the expectation that the theatre must take conventional shows. But, other considerations apart, if the local authority cannot afford a "proper" theatre, fully equipped, to take conventional shows, why not look at a form of theatre, although unconventional perhaps, but which does come within the price range that can be contemplated, and that will serve many of the purposes in the initial demand? Not all of them, of course. One that must be left out is certainly the visits of the National Theatre.

An adaptable theatre is a theatre where the stage and auditorium can be arranged in several different patterns to offer, say, theatre in the round, open stage, or proscenium stage, as required for any particular production. A multi-purpose hall is usually expected to provide at least some form of theatre, as well as facilities for dancing, exhibitions, and so on; it usually means reconciling the necessity for raised rows of seating to provide good sightlines for theatre, and a flat floor for most other purposes. Examples of small scale adaptable theatres can be seen at the Questors, and at LAMDA. The former is the home of a very enterprising and successful amateur group (of which I am proud to be a member), and the latter belongs to a dramatic training school. Something approaching a multi-purpose hall may be seen in such training colleges as St Mary's College at Twickenham, the James Graham Day Training College at Leeds, and the new hall at Leeds Grammar School. Probably the best of the mechanical adaptable theatres is the famous Loeb Theatre at Harvard, in the United States; and it leaves one with the teasing impression that the expenditure of a few more million pounds might overcome some of the limitations there. In general the idea of the multi-purpose hall is a difficult one to sort out, and the idea of an adaptable theatre is only attractive to those who like adaptable theatres. For none of its separate variants, such as proscenium theatre, thrust-stage, or theatre in the round, is likely to satisfy anyone keen on that particular form.

When faced with the demand for a multi-purpose hall, always consider that a theatre need not be used only for plays. Most conventional theatres make very acceptable cinemas (and the number of theatres that have been turned into cinemas is sufficient proof of this). A well designed theatre in the round need make no concessions to adaptability in order to be very useful for small concerts of chamber music or jazz; for fashion shows; for public meetings. If the theatre is designed along the lines of the Scarborough Library Theatre, with portable rostrum units for raising the rows of seating, a measure of adaptability may easily be attained, and end-staging, or open-staging, presented without difficulty. Further, the hall can easily be cleared, as it is in Scarborough, to provide for the conferences, banquets, exhibitions, dances and other activities that require a flat floor. The Library Theatre at Scarborough is not ideal; it was never designed as any sort of theatre in the first place. But it does present a formidably impressive case for the sort of small theatre that is easily within the means of most small towns, caters for amateur actors as well as for professional companies, and remains very much a multi-purpose hall. Finally, and very importantly, the cost of building this sort of theatre is extremely modest. It is not economic considerations that prevent towns such as Scarborough from having a good little civic theatre, though this may be one of the excuses put forward to convince a majority of people; who doesn't understand the difficulties of money? Theatre in the round will become acceptable, to councils and to actors, to playwrights and to audiences, when more of us take delight in the enjoyment of the arts and decide to break away from restrictive conventions, ignore the authority of limiting criticism; when we relish the adventure of discovering for ourselves the vast riches of the theatre.

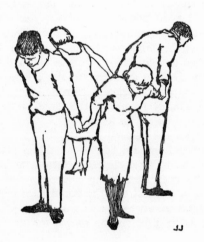

Bibliography
and
Index

Bibliography

Boyle, Walden P., *Central and Flexible Staging* (University of California Press, 1956). A well illustrated and informative little book. It deals with more than theatre in the round but is still an invaluable guide on this subject.

Halliday, F. E. *The Legend of the Rood* (Gerald Duckworth and Co. Ltd., 1955). Excerpts from the *Cornish Mystery Plays*, with a long and very interesting introduction about the Cornish Rounds and the staging of the plays. Both introduction and play extracts make fascinating reading.

Hughes, Glenn, *The Penthouse Theatre* (University of Washington Press, Seattle, 1950). The story of the first theatre in round actually built for the purpose; its antecedents, policy and philosophy, written by the man who started it and runs it.

Jones, Margo, *Theatre-in-the-Round* (Rinehart and Company, Inc., 1951). A book by the pioneer of professional theatre in the round in America, dealing with history, aesthetics and business aspects of central staging.

Southern, Richard, *The Medieval Theatre in the Round* (Faber and Faber, 1957). A scholarly attempt to reconstruct the staging of *The Castle of Perseverance* which gives the author the opportunity to say something about the Cornish rounds and even (though perhaps not fairly) about modern theatre in the round. On its main theme the book is excellent.

Villiers, André, *Le Théâtre en Rond* (Librairie Théâtrale, Paris, 1958). At present only available in French; the book ranges widely and intelligently over the history, theory and practice of central staging. It deals with the theatre in the round in Paris but is less parochial than the books by Margo Jones, Glenn Hughes and the present writer.

Index

This is a guide to persons, plays, places and publications mentioned in the book. Theatres are usually entered under place name, with the exception of London theatres. Plays can usually be found by referring either to title (*printed in italics*) or to playwright, except Shakespeare's plays which appear under title only, and a few plays and playwrights mentioned only in passing. Page numbers printed in italics refer to plates and drawings.